Being True to Life

BEING TRUE TO *Life*
Poetic Paths to Personal Growth

David Richo

SHAMBHALA
Boston & London
2009

SHAMBHALA PUBLICATIONS, INC.
Horticultural Hall
300 Massachusetts Avenue
Boston, Massachusetts 02115
www.shambhala.com

© 2009 by David Richo

9 8 7 6 5 4 3 2 1

First edition
Printed in Canada

♾ This edition is printed on acid-free paper that meets the American National Standards Institute z39.48 Standard.
♺ This book was printed on 100% postconsumer recycled paper. For more information please visit www.shambhala.com.

Distributed in the United States by Random House, Inc.,
and in Canada by Random House of Canada Ltd

Designed by Daniel Urban-Brown

Library of Congress Cataloging-in-Publication Data
Richo, David, 1940–
Being true to life: poetic paths to personal growth / David Richo.
—1st ed.
p. cm.
ISBN 978-1-59030-742-7 (pbk.: alk. paper)
1. Poetry—Authorship. 2. Self-actualization (Psychology) I. Title.
PN1059.A9R53 2009
808.1—dc22
2009010594

For my poetry teachers—the provocateurs, the guides—
Neil Topitzer, Father Jim Conefrey, Louis Mattutini, Mark Ferrer,
Donald Pierce, Ed Smallfield, Jim Wilson, Wendy Larsen,
and Emily Dickinson

You blessed me with the gift I can keep opening

Contents

Being True to Life

If you wish to receive a copy of the latest Shambhala Publications catalogue of books and to be placed on our mailing list, please send us this card, or e-mail us at: info@shambhala.com

PLEASE PRINT

Book in which this card was found

NAME

ADDRESS

CITY & STATE

ZIP OR POSTAL CODE   COUNTRY
                            (if outside U.S.A.)

E-MAIL ADDRESS

Introduction
The Healing Power of Poetry

A poem begins in delight ... and ends in a clarification of
life ... a momentary stay against confusion.

—ROBERT FROST

This book is based on the captivating and delightful idea
that writing a poem can be a powerful tool for self-discovery and
healing. In writing a poem about something that touches us we access parts of ourselves, our feelings, and our motivations that other
types of language or exploration often leave hidden. Reading or
hearing a poem can open us to new depths of understanding. In
both writing and reading poetry we are opening to our own truth
and processing it in such a way that healing and liberation can result.
Indeed, poetry—like psychological work or spiritual practice—can
help us explore and deeply understand who we are and what we are
here for.

In childhood we may have been given the gift of an Erector Set
or a dollhouse. We learned how to enjoy these gifts and we gained
many skills by using them. In school, when we memorized the
times tables, we gained information for future use. However, if we
were lucky enough to be exposed to poetry by a thoughtful teacher
and came to appreciate it, something much more powerful was going on than the gaining of skill or information. In reading it, we
were reaping the wisdom of the ages. In writing it, we were using
a tool to record and process our experiences so that meanings in
them not accessible by mere thought could be revealed. The message of this book is that the power and wisdom of poetry is still
available to us, whether we think of ourselves as poets or not.

Poetry may seem intimidating to many of us, perhaps due to our experiences having to analyze or memorize it in school. But writing a poem as part of a process of growth and healing can be intriguing and highly satisfying. Such poetry opens us up to the richness of our inner world and connects us to others, our readers.

Writing poetry to express what we are feeling, to celebrate an occasion, to show appreciation, or to follow any lead of creative imagination is a long-standing practice throughout human history. Events that fascinate or frighten us take us by the hand into valuable self-exploration. This book is intended to help you find the uncultivated poetic talents in yourself for just such an exciting journey. You may believe you have no poetic skill, yet anyone who can write words can compose a poem, just as anyone who can talk can sing and anyone who can move can dance.

In this book, we are reconnecting poetry to its healing and spiritual roots. We are discovering that there is poetry in our souls and it is located right where our growth is. We are hearing the poems of others as messages from the soul of humanity. Indeed, when we read poetry with attentiveness, it becomes a *Lectio Divina,* a divine reading, a contemplative openness to the revelations that keep coming through to us.

Composing poetry is both a psychological and a spiritual event, because the requirements for writing a poem are like those of psychological and spiritual progress. We must learn to live in the moment. We see them in new ways and focus on what is significant. We expand our freedom of imagination. We locate the many voices within us, realizing we are more than our ego. We hear and express the music and rhythms of the natural world.

In using poetry as a tool for growth and healing, we write in our own way and on any theme. We do not have to write perfectly or for publication. We accept imperfection in our craft. In fact, we write with more confidence when we are not insisting on achieving an ideal. Our only purpose is to put something on paper and then use our skills to work with it so that it says best what we feel, what we perceive, what we are passionate about. In true passion, we are not in control. Paradoxically, this surrender to what arises from within us makes us less self-conscious and more open (which are also aspects of psychological and spiritual growth). We are all already poets in the depths of ourselves—as our image-filled and wildly imaginative dreams show us!

What Is Poetry?

A poem is
a party of
Picture words
an itch for rhythms
in the shy verandah light—

Come anytime,
Rowdy to recite,
Tune-drawn—

It won't be a big bash
like at the bar down the street—
only we few desperadoes of excess,
versed in startle
and finding yet again
our own asylum from the hullabaloo.

Poetry uses words and phrases like unusual dance twists that we know we never saw before and did not quite imagine possible. As we read and write poetry, we find out how far we, too, can stretch, rotate, twirl, and reshape ourselves. We find our range of movement, our capacity to pause, and our depth of silence.

The dictionary definition of a poem may be paraphrased as "a writing in verse that is arranged in lines using rhythm, imagery, figures of speech, and sometimes rhyme to achieve an impact on our thoughts and feelings." The word *poetry* comes from the Greek word *poiein,* meaning "to make or create," with a further sense of "gathering and collecting." A poet creates by gathering and saving the images, ideas, and impressions that strike him. Then he synthesizes them and makes a poem from his own contemplations and distillations. He shares his impression through images and metaphors that contribute to the meaning he wants to convey. Thus, a poem is not only made but found, not only found but shared.

The ancient Romans around the time of Virgil referred to a poet as *vates,* that is, "a prophet or diviner." A poem is a form of divination, something that helps us look into what appears before us and see more than what ordinarily meets the eye. A poem can foresee or open us to a meaning that would not be immediately recognized. In fact, the Sanskrit word for poet is *kavi,* which also means "seer." To write poetry is to see more deeply.

Making poetry is a revolutionary act. Poems say things and present worlds that do not match the standard versions of reality to which we are accustomed or tied. A revolution frees us from attachment to what has been and the fear of what might be, in favor of what can be. To write a poem that challenges the way things are is to grow in courage through self-expression, an important contribution to our common evolutionary goals.

To read a poem is also a challenge in that we are invited to suspend our beliefs. We have to loosen up. We have to let go of our tight and circumscribed creed about what life should be and how language should work. In this way too, reading a poem is certainly a revolutionary and personally liberating exercise. Poets are not afraid to evoke a new or altogether irreverent vision for themselves and their readers. It takes freedom from fear to allow that vision to come through to us as readers—or from us as poets. Reading a poem may incite us to be rebels, since a powerful poem is an insurrection that we are invited to join.

Poetry is too intimate to be nailed down in strictly linear terms. Reading a poem is more like comprehending a multifaceted totality all at once than like following logical steps to a single conclusion. It is more like entering spirals of possibilities than like walking a straight line to a single destination.

Poetry is a mystery that ultimately defies definition, which is a clue to its spiritual scope. Therefore, whatever I affirm in this book is always open to interpretations. This is what is so wonderful about poetry: it will not sit still or stay put.

Mindfulness and Imagination

In the world of poetry, we are called on to relax our intellect and follow the pathways of mindfulness and imagination. Mindfulness means learning how to pay full attention to our moment-to-moment experience without judgment. When we are mindful, nothing in our experience is rejected as "bad"—whether it's our feelings, our thoughts, or our physical sensations. At the same time, we don't cling to any feeling or thought. We simply acknowledge whatever arises and then let it go. The exercises and practices presented in this book will help you to cultivate mindfulness as a tool for unlocking your poetic depths.

One of the most powerful ways to develop mindfulness is through sitting meditation. In mindfulness meditation, we sit and follow our breath attentively. As thoughts arise, we silently label them "thoughts," and then return our awareness to our breath. We neither suppress nor entertain any thoughts or feelings that surface. We let them arise and evaporate, like bubbles from a glass of champagne. Mindfulness meditation shows us the emptiness of ego, the illusion of self, as we see the impermanence of its thoughts and emotions. We begin to discover another dimension of ourselves where sanity and wisdom abide, the virtues that foster our personal growth and spiritual evolution. Mindfulness is an intense wakefulness, a commitment to live consciously in every moment, becoming aware even of what usually goes unnoticed, such as our breathing.

Because mindfulness involves direct seeing without judgment, it can help us approach poetry in a new way. Our fear of poetry is usually based on a judgment about ourselves. In reading a poem, for example, we might feel incapable or lacking in intelligence if we do not immediately understand what it means. This may hearken back to how we were introduced to poetry in school. When we try to compose a poem, we might immediately start to judge its literary merits and criticize or stifle ourselves. Using mindfulness, we can begin to approach poetry in a way that is far more welcoming and respectful of whatever emerges.

The practice of mindfulness can also become our entryway into the freewheeling spaciousness of imagination. In our imagination we are free to explore any images, desires, feelings, and story lines. We begin to see them all as part of our story. We begin to hold them as opportunities to grow. This leads to a kindly attitude toward our own emotions and worries. Such opening is a pathway into the full breadth of our potential as psychological and spiritual beings. We are opening to ourselves and showing more loving-kindness toward ourselves.

We know that imagining ourselves as winners, or positive visualization, helps us mobilize ourselves in the direction we desire to pursue. So imagination has the voltage to energize our potential. So much of what we are is hidden away or disowned. We usually project our untapped positive potential onto others, especially those whom we strongly admire. This keeps our own best qualities hidden. Imagining ourselves as equal to those we admire is a first step toward the actualizing of our gifts. Imagination is the antidote to disavowal.

What in meditation are distractions if we cling to them, in imagination are inroads into our creativity, and there we have the freedom to cling all we want. *We let imagination take over where mindfulness leaves off.* In mindfulness we disable the default settings of the ego: the mind-sets of fear, desire, judgment, attachment, control, and illusion. In imagination we *play* with these mind-sets creatively so that they become something new.

The neurotic ego—that is, the one driven by fear or desire—*seeks* constant entertainment to avoid really looking into itself. The imagination *uses* entertaining thoughts, memories, and feelings to access our inner world. In mindfulness we do not react to nor resist our thoughts, we simply acknowledge them and let them go. In imagination we are free to react, resist, or dwell on our thoughts in order to mine them for meanings, symbols, associations, as well as simple pleasure too. The practices in this book include visualizations and exercises that deepen our imagination and thus help us explore who we are.

When we give our imagination free rein, we are becoming poets. *Freedom* is our watchword here, freedom to express as we please, freedom to choose as we see fit, freedom to play with our illusions rather than dispel them. We come to the desk with the focus we gained from a centered meditation; we write with the freedom of a nomadic imagination. Mindfulness is our first step; release of imagination is our next step.

Like meditation, imagination is also a spiritual tool, since it grants us access not only to our personal images but to collective images and symbols. Some are from our own life and some we have inherited from ancestors from ages past. Thus, the universality and commonality of images is an emblem and indicator of the interconnectedness of all humans. Imagination is a path into that exuberantly relational style and the spiritual wisdom that flows from it. Poetry thus grants us a visa into the world of universal meanings; it combines personal and universal self-discovery.

Poetry as Therapy

Today a form of treatment called poetry therapy is used in some mental health settings for healing and growth. Patients read and write poetry to find new ways of being mindful or relaxed. Poetry can open them to new ways of coping. A poem can lead safely into realms of the unconscious that might be frightening ordinarily. Poems open the imagination to see alternatives to the status quo or to chronic suffering. In fact, every poem takes us into a parallel universe.

The realization that poetry has healing power is ancient in the human psyche. Shamans intoned poems as prayers that could bring help to the tribe or to individuals. In Egypt, as early as the fourth millennium B.C.E., poetry was inscribed on papyrus, then dissolved in a solution and ingested by patients so that their illness might subside. We recall in the Hebrew Bible that David soothed the depression of King Saul with his singing of poems in the form of psalms. A Greek physician, Soranus, who practiced in Rome in the first century C.E., was known to prescribe drama—composed of poetry—for healing. He recommended attending tragedies for his manic patients and comedies for his depressed patients.

For many centuries the connection between poetry and medicine remained in people's consciousness. Pennsylvania Hospital, founded by Benjamin Franklin in 1751, used bibliotherapy, reading and writing, as useful treatments for mental patients. Dr. Benjamin Rush, "Father of American Psychiatry," believed in the effectiveness of music and literature. In all these instances, the evocative power of poetry and the access poetry grants to emotions and catharsis were appreciated as paths to healing. We can see how poetry opens us to parts of ourselves that may not be found otherwise. In chapter 5 we will see how resolution of problems and the healing of our emotional wounds can happen as we bring our poetry to specific stresses that face us all.

Throughout this book we'll see how poetry can become a pathway of spiritual growth as well as emotional growth and healing. What do I mean by "spiritual growth"? Contacting our spirituality through poetry does not mean that we must write religious poems or haikus. Any poem can lead to awakening when approached with mindful attention. This is because its subject is the present moment, yet from it arise primordial and immortal images.

When poetry is approached as a spiritual practice, it mirrors the phases of an heroic journey, a central and universal theme in the myths of all cultures. The three phases of the heroic journey are leaving home, passing through struggles, and returning home with gifts. When we sit down mindfully to write a poem, we begin at home in our here-and-now world, with a resounding yes to what is. Then we launch out into the complex, conflicted, yet empowering reaches of our imagination, with all its fears and desires. We struggle to find the words that portray our experience. It is a struggle because, as T. S. Eliot wrote in "Burnt Norton":

> Words strain,
> Crack and sometimes break, under the burden,
> Under the tension, slip, slide, perish,
> Decay with imprecision, will not stay in place,
> Will not stay still.

Finally, we come back up with a poem that speaks to our original condition—and may at some future time speak meaningfully to others too. Writing a poem can thus take us on the same journey that a lifetime takes us on.

Indeed there are many psychological and spiritual benefits from writing poetry, including releasing ourselves from ego inhibition (holding ourselves back) and aggression (criticizing or discounting our potential skills). We inhibit and act aggressively toward ourselves when we force ourselves to be impressive or insist that our poems be perfect or be recognized by others as valuable. When poetry is our personal or spiritual practice, we give up attachment to all that and yet are open to what may result from our writing. We see our human abilities as they are and say yes to them. That yes is all we need to begin—and all we gain in the end.

We do not need Shakespeare's skill, only his enthusiasm, to write poetry. Great fervor makes us poets already, since poetry thrives on feeling. Professional skill in the craft of writing happens with time. Having passion or fervor means having an engaged, sensuous, and lively curiosity about whatever we are focusing on or whatever is beckoning to us. All of that we can achieve right now. Eventually, we may even realize that whatever we appreciate in a poet we like, we can do too—maybe not as elegantly, but certainly as passionately.

When we employ poetry as a tool for healing and transformation, we come to see that we are not only poets while we are writing; we are poets all the time. Our challenge is to remind ourselves to see with our poetic eye, the eye of yes to presence rather than to any defined or confining reality. Then when we write a poem, what comes out is real, a proclamation of our authentic voice. It sounds original, full of our own unique and lively energy, a joy to discover and release. Creativity is thus our finding in ourselves—and in the world—what Gerard Manley Hopkins called "the dearest freshness deep-down things."

Poetry makes a great contribution to our psychological work as we write about issues from our present or past. The poetic mode evokes a knowledge and insightfulness that was unconscious before we began writing. We notice how our story or predicament takes on a new significance, reveals a surprising insight, shows an unexpected depth. Writing a poem as we face any personal issue can move us into new realizations and solutions too, another surprising benefit.

A hero is one who has lived through pain, been transformed by it, and wants to share his or her gifts with others. The writing of poetry arises from any and all of those three challenges. This is because poetry can make a "Thou" of any experience. It lifts events from the condition of simple occurrences and brings them into a personal relationship to us. Human events open up into meaning, transcendence, and intimacy when there is a poem to celebrate them.

The hero is a personification of the inner urge in all of us to activate the wholeness that is in us. That is why he was born, why he goes on a journey, and how he fulfills himself. We are that hero and our poetry is most meaningful when it illumines our destiny. That destiny is to let go of our fear-based and acquisitive ego so that we can evolve into who we are when love and wisdom abound. These become the gifts we share with fellow humans. Our unique human story is an accumulation of our experiences. They all contribute to how the journey proceeds and how the world grows with us. Poetry is the perennial journal of the human story.

Poetry makes experience legible. We might join the novelist Wallace Stegner in saying that things do not expand into their full meaning, that events have not fully happened, that places have not been truly discovered until they have found a voice in poetry: "No place, not even a wild place, is a place until it has had that human attention that at its highest reach we call poetry."

Indeed, any event is incomplete until it finds some creative resonance in us. Poetry is one such instance of that personal resonance, a word that in Latin means "to sound through." In poetry, our experience sings through our words. For instance, our first child is born and we write a poem to him or about him. As our poem takes on a life of its own, we find a grander meaning than simply that of birth. His coming is a gift to us and to the world, an angelic presence among us, a challenge to us to become heart-expanded parents. All of that was in the depth of our unconscious and it came into conscious focus in the writing of our poem. Our poem arose also from the collective depths, since imagination grants us a grasp of what our forebears guessed at too. Freud wrote, "Not I, but the poets discovered the unconscious." He went further in this statement: "The mind is a poetry-making organ."

Yet poetry writing has only the *potential* to make us more psychologically whole and spiritually conscious. Artists of great skill can go through life caught in addiction or anxiety and in no way spiritually oriented. Their work may certainly tap into spiritual depths, but they do not then choose to live in accord with them. For instance, the music of Wagner is sublime and transcendent, yet he was notoriously mean-spirited and a rabid anti-Semite. Poetry does not work like magic, but it can be useful to our growth when we marry it to practice and commitment.

The awakening that is mindfulness is one of freedom from separateness. The awakening that is imagination is one of recognition of symbols and metaphors that show how realities ultimately coalesce. Some distances we can commute only by metaphor or symbol. In fact, *metaphor* in Greek means "to carry over." Poetry transports us from the one alone to the many together, a welcome demolition of the ego's illusion of separateness.

At the same time, a poem can be born of our ego and be about our ego. We do not have to let go of our ego to compose a poem. We can make our ego the subject of our poem. Just as we move from mindfulness to imagination, we can move from letting go of our ego's illusions to playfulness in recognizing them and writing from or about them.

As we saw above, in mindfulness we have no permission to indulge our fantasies; in imagination it is a requirement. This is not a loss of our spiritual consciousness but an acknowledgment that our ego remains alive and demands a hearing. Once a spiritual master has let go of ego completely, his poems are not so self-centered. Meanwhile, for all the rest of us, self-centeredness has a place in the writing of a poem, since it is our truth in this moment and leads us to existential truths too. In poetry no subject is verboten. Freedom takes precedence over letting go in this instance.

Writing a poem is also an exercise of freedom since we are released from the usual strictures of grammar and logic. We are ushered into an emancipated space in which we can visualize what is ordinarily contradictory or impossible. This happens because in poetry we can put aside grammatical and syntactical limits and, instead, fly to heights that leave rationality and logic in the dust.

Grammar is about clarity and that is important in communication. But it is also about absolute norms that can homogenize us in such a way that we may fail to find our own voice and all its stirring peculiarities. Poetry is a declaration of independence from the uniform world, from rules that bind us, from rulers that lord it over us.

The literary critic Harold Bloom commented that Shakespeare upgraded the English language and showed us its range while at the same time showing us how to be more human. Plato did the same in Greek, as Cicero did in Latin. Their upgrading of language happened in the context of their offering an upgraded way of being more richly human. There is a direct connection between expanding our range of language and expanding our understanding and wisdom.

Discovering the Poet Within

Something kept itself alive after grammar school. It is the poet within. She lives in utter liberty of imagination, shorn of the restrictive mind-sets of linguistic correctness. This is how new vectors of being and perception appear in that center of the human soul where all life's radii meet. There and only there are we abundantly ourselves. These lines of Walt Whitman (from his poem "One hour to madness and joy" in *Leaves of Grass*, 1900) celebrate the combining of our voice and our abundance:

> To have the gag removed from one's mouth!
> To have the feeling to-day or any day I am sufficient as I am.

Poetry is a field, like a field of gravity, without strict or restricting boundaries. We are suspended in space, upheld only by artistry. We are not in the safe container of syllogisms or syntax that can be trusted to explain the world to us. Sometimes poetry, even our own, defies full explanation. Indeed, good poems are bottomless. They never yield their meaning fully, perhaps not even to the poet. They are inexhaustible, like Shakespeare, like the art in Rome, or like the love in our hearts.

Those of us who loved poetry from the moment we were introduced to it may have noticed that we were either alone or in the minority. Most of our fellow students were perhaps not so turned on. They may have found poetry useless, boring, intimidating, or incomprehensible. All through life, we have probably noticed that we poetry lovers have remained on the outskirts. Yet, to be marginalized leads to a clearer sense of our own distinctive identity. The less we fit into a parochial and safely conventional society, the more able are we to come upon our own truth and the more likely are we to write our own poems and to understand those of our fellow poets. Poets bud when they find authority in their words, no matter how unaccepted, misunderstood, invalidated, or unnoticed by the conventional world.

In our day, poetry is still in the subculture. It has not made it to the top of the list of priorities. It is the "extra," the warm moment at the presidential inauguration, the poignant cry at the offbeat poetry reading, the toast at the wedding. But it is not yet as impactful or as *necessary* to us as our consumerism. This is quite different from ancient times, when the poetic voice was thought to be such a powerfully revolutionary force that Plato, who loved poetry, suggested that all poets be banished from the ideal and well-ordered state.

Nonetheless, poetry is experiencing at least a partial rebirth. We find poetry readings and slams (or competitions) everywhere. We listen to songs, every one of which is a poem. We browse the Internet and find hundreds of poems. The margins are wider now than in our school days.

Excitement about songs is the equivalent of a love of poetry, since the lyrics are poems. The motivation of the thousands that attend rock concerts is not only about the appeal of music but of poetry too.

In this new environment, we can learn so much by listening to other poets who bravely voice their feelings and realizations. They offer new forms of self-help, since we find mirroring of our own experience in their words and challenges to widen our own souls in the confessions they make. We hone our own voice as we listen to those of others like—or unlike—us.

What follows in this book is an invitation to you to try your hand at writing poetry and to open your mind to reading it in a new way. There are many exercises that may help you write better than ever and appreciate others' poems more deeply. You will, as well, discover yet another inspiring and surprising path to psychological growth and spiritual practice. Finally, and most encouraging of all, you will be set free from what may be a stunted imagination and you will watch breathlessly as your soul opens into a sky.

> The dancing feet...
> The songs and vibrating rhythms
> Of our dancing Lord,
> Imitate them all and bliss is yours.
> —Mahadevi, twelfth century (my translation)

I

Discovering Your Truth

> Whether or not we are aware of it, there is nothing of which we are more ashamed than of not being ourselves, and there is nothing that gives us greater pride and happiness than to think, to feel, and to say what is ours.
>
> —ERICH FROMM

The most exciting part of finding out who we are is discovering our own uniqueness, who we are "outside the box," beyond the categories in a Psychology 101 textbook. In our inimitable singularity, there is an infinite range of possibility that cannot be tied to any one description of what it means to be human or healthy. Just as our fingerprints are one-of-a-kind, so is our identity. Each of us is a once-only articulation of what humans can be. We are rare, unmatched, mysterious. This is why the quality of openness is so crucial to our self-discovery. We cannot know ourselves by who we think we are, who others take us to be, or what our driver's license may say. We are fields of potential, some now actualized, most not yet. Poetry goes to that quarter of what humanness is about. It is what openness looks like on a page.

There is a natural and inviolable tendency in things to bloom into whatever they truly are in the core of their being. This process is sometimes called *autopoiesis,* which means "self-creation" or "self-organization." We come into the world with certain talents and gifts. These seek activation in our own unique voice and in our own manner. All we have to do is align ourselves with what wants to happen naturally and put in the effort that is our part in helping it happen.

The object-relations therapist Margaret Mahler wrote, "There is in us an innate given, a thrust toward individuation, which seems to continue during the entire life cycle." The drive in us to self-actualize is irresistible and fully connected to the unflappable urge of the universe to evolve through each of us. Something bigger than us wants us to evolve. If as children we were parented with what I call the "five A's"—attention, acceptance, appreciation, affection, and allowing—we blossom more readily into the people we were meant to be, because we have a sense of our own self-worth and are continually activating our powers. If we were not nurtured with the five A's of love, we are challenged to do the work it takes to heal and advance ourselves. Writing a poem can be part of that practice. (Later we will revisit the five A's with a specific example and its application to writing a poem.)

Poetry is what words want to do so that they can release far-reaching realizations—or gentle intimations—about the vast uncharted terrain in ourselves. Our poems are how we find ourselves attentively, acceptingly, appreciatively, affectionately, and with full allowing of all that we are and can be. In other words, poetry is a pathway of autopoiesis.

Finding Your Authentic Voice

Finding our authentic voice is a path to self-realization, and our poems offer a wonderful way of making the journey. This is because all that we do and all that happens to us can be the subject of poetry, with nothing left out. Poems arise from every chapter of any biography. A poem may articulate an emotional experience that is attractive or repulsive. In that sense, a poem makes all life events and predicaments equal and fosters equanimity in the face of life's blows or kudos.

Success in life is finding and declaring our own truth in our own way. Presenting our authentic voice in our poems is of greater value than having our poems published. Giving precedence to articulating our true voice flows from contentment with who we are right now. A poem is one way our true identity opens, and it is a joy to let that happen. This is how our writing a poem to contemplate or explore our experience can be life-giving, that is, produce more of the life that we are.

When we write a poem, we may be surprised at the variety of voices that emerge from us. Indeed, there are many voices in us. Some are unique to us, arising from our own life story. Others are universal, since they reflect archetypes from the collective human story. The creative process is an activation of many archetypal images and an elaboration of these images into metaphors about ourselves and our world. This is just how it is in the evolutionary lifetime of beings like us who are too vast to be depicted in portraits. We are galleries, after all.

When our sense of ourselves is tied to one story from our past, our full voice cannot emerge. When we work through our past issues, we discover new unexplored sectors in ourselves. This is how our psychological work on ourselves can contribute to the growth of our imagination. A one-note story about who we are keeps us limited in range so that we are less likely to sing with what John Keats in "Ode to a Nightingale" called "full-throated ease."

Finding our own voice includes the discovery of the darker continents in our psyche, which we may have only guessed were there, and naming them, as explorers do. One of the scariest universal human archetypes is the negative shadow, the side of ourselves that may be unacceptable to the conventional world, the side that may be unappealing even to ourselves. It is unconscious and disavowed, but writing a poem often accesses that darkness and evokes it into the light. Then we can work with it and find ways for it to become an ally. Creativity and imagination are our midwives in this process.

We have a positive shadow too, a side of us that holds an incalculable treasury of gifts, talents, and potentials that we may not believe could possibly be in us. A poem can gain access to those heretofore disowned and recondite riches. Thus our shadow is the mother lode of our creativity. *What lies waiting in my darkness beyond what I allow myself to think?*

Poetry writing can release both creative shadow sides of us and produce images that reveal them or let them finally speak. In this way, writing a poem can correct the one-sidedness of our ego by exposing and integrating what has been overlooked in our personality. We do not plan this. Our writing of a poem kindly deceives us into a more remote precinct of ourselves. The pen draws some unconscious data up into consciousness. Now we are hearing from some of our disparate but native voices. This is yet another example of how personal discovery and what happens in the composing of poetry are intertwined.

Henry David Thoreau said that if one sits in a clearing long enough and quietly enough, soon all the animals come out of the woods and present themselves. When we chase after experience or run away from it, we miss our chance at such a festive visitation. This friendly event is just what can happen in mindfulness and imagination. We sit in the here and now and then open ourselves to the images that want to greet us. We meet the many faces in us that want to be in our album. We sit to invite; we sit to welcome; we sit to include.

We can see our inner life as a playroom in which every energy and archetype of humanity can find camaraderie and even amusement. Once we let go of the importance of like and dislike, we begin to include all the selves that we are, each depending on the causes and conditions around us. We let go of the idea of a single self at the controls, and our true identity reveals itself to be an amphictyony, a word referring to a group of states that cooperate, especially in the care of temples and shrines. Our true presence is indeed a sacred marriage.

Discovery and integration of our submerged selves is an empowerment and a fortification, because now we know ourselves all the way rather than only halfway—the half that the world approves. Now we can bravely acknowledge our fears or longings no matter how unappealing they may seem to us or how they may repulse others. Our poems can then become our emancipation proclamations. This may be what Pablo Picasso meant when he said, "Art helps us seize power by giving a form to our terrors and desires."

Writing poetry is full permission to find, explore, and confront our true selves—quite a challenge. Once we are free of constraint, inhibition, or ignorance of our own truth, we can open fearlessly to who we are. This is liberation from the limits of our constricted ego. We have nothing to fear in what may arise; it is all rising into the light so that it can become useful for the revelation of our own truth. The poet Matthew Arnold wrote, "Poetry is nothing less than the most perfect speech of man, that in which he comes nearest to being able to utter the truth."

Our core self is the reality of us. It is often not safe to show, yet it waits to be found by us and others and embraced with the five A's. That embrace makes for safety. Poems are so often the best vehicle for an exposition of the true self. We are not on guard, that is, caught in the default setting of the scared or defensive ego. We open ourselves from the heart, the locus of our spiritual powers.

To write poetry is certainly initiatory as we go through the pain of hunting for the words that can say exactly what we mean. The result of our conscientiousness is access to a world beyond our ordinary limits, where just the right words and images fly in. Indeed, the twentieth-century American poet Wallace Stevens said that a poem is "a meteor." To live through struggles in life is also initiatory. The result of our conscientious work on ourselves to become more psychologically fit grants access to a world beyond our usual limits, where meteors abound!

Becoming a Fair and Alert Observer

> Now I will do nothing but listen,
> To accrue what I hear into this song ....
> —WALT WHITMAN, "SONG OF MYSELF"

Writing a good poem—a poem that is meaningful, healing, or liberating—requires a candidness about ourselves and a loyalty to our experience. We let ourselves appear just as we are with all our gifts and limitations. We avoid the tendency to sand down the rough edges of reality in order to make it cosmetically pleasing. We give up trying to moralize or push our point of view onto others. We avoid the tendency to tie things together with a bow rather than to say yes to the unkemptness we may be observing in reality. Finally, we do not simply copy what we see but give our own take on it. Then we are witnesses, not thinkers; we are "wide receivers," not "tight ends."

Our minds work in many ways. Two ways that stand out are thinking and witnessing. For instance, we may think about learning to swim, then study our options, and finally arrive at a well-thought-out decision about which swimming class to take. At another time, while crossing a bridge, we might see a person drowning. There is no time to think. We simply see and jump in the water to save the person in crisis, whether or not we have swimming skills.

Our thinking mind conceptualizes a specific take on reality and then may present it as a truth. "Message poems" can come from that quarter. The style of our witnessing mind is awareness. When we sit in meditation, focusing on our breath and not entertaining thoughts, we are not thinkers but witnesses.

Mindfulness increases witness consciousness. Then we can see all that happens to us without an attachment to permanent definitions but rather with an openness to what wants to come through to us in the present moment. This is precisely the requisite and preparatory course in the writing of poetry from our own reality but with no attempt to force our view on others. Writing poetry helps us grow, because it is an art of contact. It does this by preferring here-and-now experience to formulated message, immediate awareness to lengthy conceptualizing.

We are ready to release our imagination into poetry as we empty ourselves of the need to be sure about things, to take refuge in the tried and true, to follow accustomed pathways, or to get the rightness of our point across. It is not that having a message is wrong in any way. It is appropriate in any form of communication, including poetry. It is problematic when we are forcing our view on the reader rather than simply sharing it. Here, too, we see how the rules for a good poem are the same as those for a healthy style of communication in general.

Mindfulness helps us in all this because it opens our perception to the present moment rather than miring us in conceptions about it. Writing is entering the reality of something like an explorer, with no preconceived notions of what the landscape will look like. We are brave enough to remove what the poet Shelley called "the film of familiarity" so that we can see something new and newly.

Freud recommended that the analyst maintain "free-floating [that is, evenly spread] attention" during the therapy hour. This means paying attention *but without any single focus*. We may thereby allow our consciousness to move openly without stopping anywhere in particular. Such free-floating attentiveness is a form of mindfulness since it fosters a limitless, moving, spacious presence rather than a narrow, ego-driven focus. We let in what is but with no attempt to debate or evaluate. We simply float and flow with what is happening, internally or externally. Freud's intuition about the usefulness of free-floating attention can help us expand both our spiritual practice and our entering into the poetic mind.

> When you finally get it, there's no place for it but in a poem.
>
> —Wu Pen (779–843)

EXERCISES

Getting Started with Poetry

We will not be discouraged by anything except not writing at all. We will be successful when we remain committed to continual practice. After all, in the *Bhagavad Gita* Krishna has encouraged us to "let go of the fruits of action but never the action itself."

Jumping in and writing a poem, no matter how amateurish the result may look, may prove more valuable than waiting for inspiration or studying poetic forms. Here are some helpful exercises to get you started.

———

Choose an image or object that appeals to you. Apply the "five A's" of mindfulness to it: Pay close *attention* to the object with no attempt to change or improve it. *Accept* the object as itself, not attempting to jimmy it into a position that fits your agenda or projections. Let yourself feel an *affection* for and an *appreciation* of the object. Finally, *allow* it to speak to you in its own words.

For example, you might be looking at an apple and notice it has a gash, is not so red, or is lying on its side rather than straight up. While you're holding this apple in your awareness, you might recall that you like Macintosh more than Golden Delicious apples. Let go of your preferences and any need to rearrange the apple and simply let it be what it is, as it is. In this mindful space, you are ready to hear what the apple itself has to say to you. Then write what you hear in lines not paragraphs, phrases not sentences.

Sit silently for a few moments. Silence does not mean that we are mute. It is an attitude of listening to our inner world while we are not talking or getting lost in thoughts. Silence is a path to witnessing and becoming more aware. *Breathe in while forming the image of opening your mind. Breathe out with the image of relaxing your body.* Do this several times and then write automatically without thinking, using short, poetic lines. Then rewrite as you see fit.

Try a walking meditation in which you stride slowly, rhythmically, and deliberately with no specific destination. A walk in nature with attention to what you see, hear, and smell can be a form of walking meditation. Compose a three-line poem that reflects anything that you felt, noticed, or learned. For example, you noticed a pine tree standing alone and thought of how alone you feel sometimes. You were touched by a sense of courage in how the pine tree stood. You write, "Pine tree, you look brave standing alone." You can also write it this way:

Pine tree,
You look brave
Standing alone.

Later, you can play with these short lines. For example, the word *pine* might make you think of the word *pining*. You also like the *o* sound in *alone;* it seems soulful. So you change *brave* into *bold* since it, too, has the *o* sound. Now your poem looks like this:

Pine not pining,
Alone and bold.

Consider these words by Wallace Stevens, from his poem "Notes toward a Supreme Fiction":

Perhaps
The truth depends on a walk around a lake,
...a rest
In the swags of pine-trees bordering the lake.*

————

Freud said, "The body never lies." We can trust our bodies to bring us authentic news about who we are and are becoming, what others mean to us or can mean, what the world is doing to us or how it asks us to help it evolve. Pay close attention to your body and its sensations. Notice how each of your five senses reacts to the world, to others, and to events. Keep note of these reactions and build poems from them.

Wallace Stevens wrote, "With my whole body I taste these peaches." Inspiration can arise from our bodily reactions to everyday events. Carl Jung referred to the body as "the densest part of the unconscious." Thus, we can begin to appreciate bodily sensations, feelings, even symptoms, as sources of inspiration, a spirit of creativity breathing through us.

For some people, stopping and paying attention to the body can be daunting. We might find that our body has become a storehouse of painful memories. Or perhaps we feel numbed by our life experiences. It's worth noticing that the body combines opposites: it holds tension but is also a *resource* for healing, as happens when taking deep breaths relaxes us. We no longer have to think of our bodies as a repository of painful memories. We can discover that

————

* From *The Palm at the End of the Mind,* ed. Holly Stevens (New York: Vintage Books, 1972).

it offers equal opportunities for healing. Writing about what our body is feeling or telling us opens that treasury.

Notice your sensations and bodily reactions and write short poems that identify the felt sense and felt mood of them, a bodily resonance that describes what you feel. Do this with no motivation to change anything, only to report the many dimensions of your experience.

———

An important path to finding out who we are is knowing what we really want. Here is a simple exercise that may help you get there. Ask yourself these three questions: What do I want to start doing? What do I want to stop doing? What do I want to keep doing? By answering these three questions, you are auditing your life to see if it is in keeping with what you really want to be. Answer each question in your journal, writing in any way at all. Look at your entry three days later and revise it if necessary so that each of your responses is authentic—neither too grand nor too minimal.

Two days later, rewrite each answer so that it becomes a *challenge* to you and is specific about how your life can change to reflect your deepest needs, values, and wishes accurately. One day after that, rewrite your journal entry in poetic lines and as empowering affirmations. Then place your poem in a place that will be visible so you can remind yourself to look for ways to put them into practice. You can trust that synchronicities will occur, that is, challenges will arise that match your affirmations and call you on your commitment. The universe has joined you in your evolutionary plan. Your path comes to meet you; you don't have to wait to find it.

> Authentic tidings of invisible things,
> Of ebb and flow, and ever-enduring power ...
> —WILLIAM WORDSWORTH, "THE EXCURSION"

2

Writing the Poems Inside You

The farthest horizons of our hopes and fears are cobbled by
our poems, carved from the rock experiences of our daily lives.

—AUDRE LORDE

Our poems do not have to be considered expert or artful by
others in order to be of value. We do not set out to write a high-quality
poem but rather to tap into what is true and real for us. At the same
time, we can benefit from pointers on improving our way of writing.
We do this so that we can better express what we are feeling and so that
we can be better understood by others. What follows in this chapter
may help us achieve more clarity. In each instance, we make the connection between our psychospiritual work and the improvement of
our writing. This is how it can become an adjunct to growth and an
expression of our progress toward the release of our fully realized selves.

Our progress in the skill of writing poetry certainly mirrors our
progress in personal development. This is because as our lives become
less complex, we write more simply. As mindfulness takes precedence
over story lines, we write with more economy and clarity. As our relationships become more intimate, our writing is more unabashedly
personal and candid. As our stress levels diminish, we focus on our
themes and produce poems with coherence and impact.

Guidelines for Creating Poetry for Growth and Healing
1. Write It Any Old Way
"Any old way" is one possible description of how we begin the work
of becoming healthy psychologically. We acknowledge that we are

beginners, so we are willing to look foolish and awkward at times as we practice becoming healthier. For instance, our self-esteem may have suffered because we have been submissive and passive in our daily transactions. We make a commitment to assertiveness in our speech and manner. At first, we stumble and stammer, but we are willing to do something badly rather than not at all, so we stay with it. We say something, however timidly, to show others that we have an opinion and a right to express it. We do not yet say it as Thomas Jefferson would have, but we know we can always keep revising. Our poetry writing has certainly taught us that.

In the story of Rumpelstiltskin, the main character is required to turn straw into gold. Eventually the straw does turn to gold, so the straw and gold were actually one to begin with. This is an alchemical metaphor. It also presents a combination of opposites. Our first version of a poem may seem like straw—of little value—but it has the makings of gold, something of value. It takes faith to write a poem. We have to believe in possibilities, as Emily Dickinson says: "I dwell in Possibility—/ A fairer House than Prose."

Stanley Kunitz, looking at the poems of his student Louise Glück, said that they were "awful." Then he added that she was nonetheless a poet! We may not like what we write; we may not find an audience that appreciates it. That does not mean we are not poets. Our only job description is practice.

Don't try to make your poem perfect from the start. Begin writing haphazardly, sloppily, amateurishly, in any old way. Aristotle in *Poetics IV* wrote, "Persons starting with this natural gift developed by degrees their special aptitudes, till their rude improvisations gave birth to poetry."

When writing a poem, it is important not to wax poetic. Don't decorate reality with frills. Words in a poem, like lovers, are to be chosen very carefully. Beware of using too many stage dressings. At the same time, the epiphany moment in a poem is usually lyrical. When lyric beauty comes through our words naturally, we appreciate that and make room for it. Then our writing gains a musical power. No one can object to that, any more than we can be scolded for adding honey to our yogurt.

It is crucial not to repeat the point that a poem makes nor to make the point too obviously. It is best to allow the reader to draw a conclusion from your words rather than for you to hammer it home. Restating dilutes the punch, and a hammer leaves one punch-drunk rather than awake and looking for more. Let the readers look for your or their own meaning. Don't try to convince the reader of something. Let her draw her own conclusions.

PRACTICES

Try writing a poem with words or phrases you come upon spontaneously in the course of the day, for example, on signs, labels, advertisements, bills. This "found language" uses words that seem to have little potential for poetry yet can stir your unconscious and automatically produce something that has significance and relevance.

For instance, here are some phrases from a bottle of fruit juice: *blend, tangy, refreshing, fully organic, vitamin-rich, natural.* You may first list the words and add to them so that they become phrases. The first thought in the first phrase can set a tone or theme. For instance, *blend* can become "I keep trying to blend in." Now your poem will be about your comfortableness, or lack of it, in the social world. Or you can simply write in a way that is playful and not so obviously personal or psychological. The fun and creativity are therapeutic in any case. You do not have to use all the words and you can change the meanings and contexts all you want.

Write a "cut-up poem," one in which you cut out words and phrases from poems in magazines, then reassemble them in ways that seem creative to you. Notice how your voice joins with that of the poets and new themes emerge from the combination of their voices and yours.

Write a nonsense poem or nursery rhyme that strings together images and thoughts with no logical sequence. This exercise shows how poetry can be fun and surprising in what it generates spontaneously. That spontaneity is a feature of becoming healthier since it leads to more ease in reevaluating and then letting go of what has become so deadly serious in our lives.

2. Be Open to Inspiration

So much of our work on ourselves, both psychologically and spiritually, is to allow rather than to accomplish. Emma Jung (the wife of Carl Jung) writes in *The Holy Grail*, "An inner wholeness presses its still unfulfilled claims upon us." Once we trust that wholeness is in us, we put our accent on opening to what wants to come through us, opening to inspiration. The word *inspiration* is based on the Greek word for "enthusiasm," which literally means "God within." When we listen to the voice that speaks through us, we are hearkening to a divine reality. This is how poetry is a revelation, the liturgy of the word.

We believe there is abundance in us and that our work is not to plant it but to harvest it. The spiritual richness of our psychological work then becomes clear: We are receiving a revelation from the Sinai of the soul about who we really are and what our calling is. Like Moses, we have only to stand in awe and watch the fire.

A poem of ours is like a child of ours, related to us, from us, but with a mind of its own. Let the poem breathe on its own. The more time you take writing a poem, the more attention you devote to it, the deeper you go into yourself and your meanings and the more the poem speaks to you in its own—that is, your own—voice.

William Wordsworth explained how a particular poem took shape for him: In 1843 he described a large thorn on a plant that he had passed by often. But after a storm it stood out more sharply and he noticed it in a more focused way, seeing contours in it that he had not noticed before. He reports saying to himself, "Can I by some invention do as much to make this thorn permanently an impressive object, as the storm has made it to my eyes at this moment?" The artistry of the storm on the thorn became his inspiration. He then wrote the poem "The Thorn" with great ease, as if from an epiphany.

We let our poem unfold, emerge, appear, result, happen, crawl out from what we see or feel in the moment. Then we find out what we wanted to say, a revelation of what was already in us, waiting for its chance to make a personal appearance. It is easy to see that this advice for composing a poem applies, as well, to life itself.

PRACTICES

Choose a story from your own life. The story becomes your inspiration to write a prose poem, a paragraph or more that has the qualities of a poem by reason of its economical, figurative, and rhythmic language, but is in prose, that is, paragraph, form. As you pare the story down and find rhythms in it, you simultaneously reframe it. This new frame shows its authentic essence and possibly its humor, elements that you may not have noticed before.

"To write a poem, follow any thread but don't pull it," was the sound advice of the poet William Stafford. Any person, place, mood, feeling, thing, image, thought, predicament, fiction, illusion, neurosis, or nonsense can inspire a poem. Look around the room you are in or look outdoors at nature. Stay with whatever you are looking at or feeling right now without attempting to force it into something or to look for a message in it. Let the subject lead you, become what it chooses to become, begin and end as it may. Write as if you were recording what you see or feel. Then shape it into poetic lines. Revise it by adding the elements of poetry: rhythm, sensuous images, figures of speech, economical language, and uninhibited, imaginative ways of handling your topic.

3. *Maintain the Economy*

Economy of words is about making space. The Tibetan Buddhist teacher Chögyam Trungpa said that we do not have to create space to make a cup. It happens all by itself once the cup is made. Spaciousness in ourselves happens as we open ourselves to all the options life offers, all the givens it challenges us to face. To do this means that we open mindfully to reality, free of fear. Poetry is for those who are unafraid to feel and eager to show all.

Mary Oliver refers to economical poetry as a "coiled spring, waiting to release its energy in a few clear phrases." I recall a movie from
my childhood in which Betty Grable, a star who was famous for her
beautiful shape and legs, was showing her director the gown she
planned to wear for an upcoming show. The dress sported many frills
and feathers and covered her from neck to toe. The director immediately ripped off large swatches of it so that her bodice and legs could
be fetchingly exposed. In poetry writing we practice the same kind of
trimming in order to show the parts that are most appealing. Emerson
commented, "Poetry teaches the enormous force of a few words."

Look for and omit excessive adjectives, adverbs, and articles, trite
phrases, forced rhyme, padding that sounds pleasing but does not
add to the power of the poem. Say the most while using the least.
Economy in our writing is a spiritual practice since, as we saw above,
it creates space. Such is the emptiness from which all emerges. The
spaces say something just as well as the words do. Let your poem be
thereby truly creative, making something from nothing.

At the same time, it is important not to make a poem so trim
that the reader will not understand it. The task in a poem is to use
words that say all that has to be said in a way that both leaves room
for readers to add their own perspectives and discloses the full pan-
orama of your idea. Use many, too many, words in one version of
your poem and then judiciously decide which to omit as you move
toward the final version. Experiment with writing longer lines. The
length of a line and the number of words has nothing to do with
economy; only unnecessary words define that. Giving too many
details in a poem can be boring and distracting to the reader. But
carefully chosen details that illuminate the theme can elicit feeling.

A final word on rhyming: Use it only when it is not sing-song
or when it makes your poem superficial. The best rhyme helps the
poet find a surprising and unexpected direction or connection.

PRACTICE

Take a recent event that has led to your having strong feelings. Write
a phrase describing the event, brief and unadorned, as a headline, for

instance, "I was rejected by Alice." Draw a circle around the head-line phrase. Now draw four concentric circles around that circle. In the first one, next to the center circle, write your belief about the event, for instance, "I am unworthy of being liked." In the second, write a judgment about Alice: "I blame her for being unfair." In the third, write a fantasy that makes you feel you are in control: "I can change her mind." In the fourth, write what you plan to do: "I will be open to discussing our relationship if she accepts me. I will reject her and not forgive her if she does not accept me."

On a separate sheet, write a line for each of the five entries that summarizes and expands on it: the original event, the belief, the judgment, the fantasy, and the plan. These are the five themes that we embroider around most events in life. They are story elements that keep us one step removed from reality. Now sit mindfully contemplating the original experience you had with Alice. When you are calm, begin to cross off one line after another, beginning at the bottom. This leaves you with one line: the original event. Under that write a line that describes the reality of your own bare pain about what happened, for example, "I was rejected / I am sad." That is the poem.

———

Here's another variation of this exercise. In this one, you track your train of thought by noticing how it began and then catching yourself spinning the mental story that followed. For instance, you woke up this morning feeling sad and lonely. Your first reaction was to give yourself a reason: "I feel bad because I do not have a friend or partner." This became generalized: "No one wants to be with me." Then a criticism arose to make matters worse: "I am not interesting or likable enough." The story continued along the familiar track of self-negation until your sense of loneliness increased and became despair.

The healing practice is to go back to the first line of the story: "I woke up sad and lonely." This is the headline, the only real experience; the rest was self-generated editorializing. You can jump from that train of thought by staying with the original experience. You do this by entering it with a ruthless willingness to be in it as it is, with no need to explain or evade it. Your breathing and mindfulness practices come to the rescue here. You stop and spend a few moments just breathing and allowing your experience to be what it is.

You notice that you do have a way of living through your painful feelings. The realization that you have courage becomes more important to you than whether you are alone today. It can even replace the original feelings with a calm joy and pride in yourself. You have said yes to a doleful reality without letting it get to you, the very definition of equanimity.

Writing, immediately and spontaneously, especially after something happens, is an alternative to thinking, so it is a way of being true to life rather than logic. There our unconscious may surprise, stun, or startle us. What could be more useful to awakening?

―――

These last two exercises *open* you to your authentic feelings, unbuffered by thoughts and beliefs. In working with your feelings this way you are more likely to envision―that is, *imagine*―ways you can heal yourself by letting go of ego obsessions about whether others include or exclude you. Now you are ready to bring all this into the practice of *loving-kindness*. Write lines that extend welcoming love to yourself, to those you love, to the person who rejected you recently, to all who have rejected you over the years, and finally to all humanity. Extend compassion, joy, and equanimity with further lines. This practice makes love *universal* in its extent and turns your personal experience into an outreach to all humanity. Your poem has now expanded, as you have.

Finally, put the lines together and shave off any unnecessary words, a mindful holding of your original experience. This is a spiritual activity, since you have transitioned from an ego-enclosed experience into a soul-opening event. You then *universally widened* your circle of love and concern by including all humanity in your personal experience.

4. Consider Words, Lines, and Forms

> ... the quality to bring forth what lies slumbering forever
> ready in all words.
>
> ―WALT WHITMAN, *Leaves of Grass*

Becoming specific is part of becoming psychologically well, since it is an addressing of whatever our issue may be. This is a facing of reality rather than having our back to it. As we use the words that tell it as it is, we rest on the "what is," the reality of life and its givens, rather than on fantasies about how it can be ensured or reversed. This means experiencing life, predicaments, events just as they are without the embroidering mind-webs of judgment, blame, coercion, attachment to outcome, fantasy, and projections that help us escape the full wallop of reality. We do this, for instance, when we feel our grief about a loss without judging ourselves for it or attempting to control its duration. As a result, we grow in self-esteem. In reality, we are entering the realm of our abundant selves where anything goes, in every sense of that phrase.

In writing a poem, cultivate a healthy discomfort with abstraction or complexity. Use words that tell what you feel rather than words that sound poetic in the conventional sense but may be so abstract or obscure that they fail to make an impact. Wrestle with words until you find the ones that reflect your experience in the most earthy way possible. Anglo-Saxon words do this better than Latin-based words. For instance, "She left my home," using Anglo-Saxon words, sounds more powerful than "She vacated my habitation," using Latin-based words.

At the same time, use language that evokes an image or a mood. For instance, the phrase *left behind* does not say as much as *marooned,* a word that has more sonority as well. A colorful choice of words likewise says so much more than simple exposition. For instance, Emily Dickinson's line "There is no frigate like a book" has more richness than "There is no boat like a book." The general denotation of *frigate* and *boat* is the same, but the word *frigate* has connotations of swashbuckling adventure and adds a more appealing sound and rhythm. We feel we are going somewhere new and risky, not just being transported from one place to another, which is as much cargo as the word *boat* can carry. We can also imagine how the poem would change if she had used *schooner* or *yacht* or *canoe.*

The word *verse* refers to a line of poetry. It can also refer to any superficial or trivial metrical writing that is distinguished from poetry because of its inferior quality. Verse attempts to be lofty but uses so many, usually trite, adjectives and adverbs, and is often so self-centered or maudlin, that its point—a shallow one at best—makes no lasting or strong impact on us as readers. Here is an example:

> Fluffy clouds of enticing cotton candy
> Sail gently and sweetly across
> The rolling blue waves of majestic sky.

We are not drawn to reread this bombastic verse because we do not hear an authentic voice, only hackneyed phrases, such as might appear on a greeting card. Our human path is grounded in the here-and-now gritty predicaments we live in. Verse is the language of the superficial ego. Poetry is the language of the mature ego that honors basic reality and uses words to depict it rather than cosmeticize it.

Pay attention to your line breaks. They are like meditative breaths. Their purpose is to slow the reader down so that he or she can focus on what you are saying. In this sense, they are your directions to the reader. What we do in writing a poem is certainly like what we do in breathing: Each line is a breath, and spaces on the page are timed breaths. An inner ordering is happening as you write a poem, like the order in a melody. Poems are also aesthetically pleasing, shapely, because of their lines and how they look on the page.

PRACTICE

In this exercise, write your sentences in a list rather than as paragraphs.

Write a description in four sentences of the city you live in. Write three sentences about what you are doing there. Choose what you most like about it, such as tree-lined streets, and write two sentences on that. Now describe your feelings about the city in one sentence.

Rename the original image, your home city, as "my life," and rewrite your sentences in accord with that change: who or where you are as a person now, what you are doing in your life, what you most like about yourself, and what you are feeling about yourself. Give your poem a title, but not until after you have written it.

Take the ten sentences you have written and condense them into an "etheree." This form was created by an Arkansas poet named Etheree Taylor Armstrong. The etheree consists of ten lines of un-metered verse focusing on one idea, the first line having one syl-lable, each succeeding line adding a syllable, with the total syllable count being fifty-five. Below is an example in which I gave myself two more challenges: I used only one-syllable words and no Latin-based ones. Add these challenges if you want to.

And By a Sleep to Say

> Sleep.
> Ah, more
> Stop than start.
> Will I drowse here
> All the way down night
> Or bolt up big-eyed waked
> Scared to nod to lord of dreams
> Who dares me drift and dares me dark?
> Or can't I bear the *rest*—the far fall,
> Deep gulf—that feels so like a death of me?

5. Be Very Personal but Not Too Subjective

Our challenge in forming healthy relationships is to remain self-disclosing and continually communicative. When we become se-cretive or elusive, our partner loses contact with our heart and may have the sense of being excluded or abandoned.

In addition, when we notice ourselves hiding, we might ask if we are fearing the implications of intimacy, radical openness, and genuine sharing. As we become healthier, we want to be known as we are and we want our motivations to be seen for what they are. Then a dialogue without blame or shame can begin, and we welcome it. Writing our poems in ways that reach out to the reader presents the same set of challenges as reaching out to someone we love. Both take vulnerability.

The attitude of welcoming helps us see the oft-hidden mean-ings in things and events. What attracts our attention becomes the pathway into meaning. The Homeric verb *mnaomai* means both "to draw attention to" as well as "to woo." Perhaps there is something in what enlists our focus that is *affectionate* toward us, wooing us in some touching way. In this sense all that happens in a partnership can be love poems, outreaches to us, evocations of our powers to be loving. Levels of significance arise spontaneously and we see into the heart of what our love is really about and cherish it all the more. What else would a poem or a relationship be for?

A poem is meant to be *personal* rather than subjective. When a poem is personal, readers can feel the presence of the poet, because his or her unique feelings and mood come through to them. This may lead readers to see themselves and their own similar experience in the poem. When a poem is *subjective,* it contains information knowable only to the poet and allows no point of entry for readers. Such a poem makes a statement but without communicating, like using a foreign language. Readers then lose confidence in their ability to grasp a meaning and feel shut out. Meaningful poetry establishes a connection by being true to life rather than preventing such a connection by being cryptic.

At the same time, some of our poems are just for ourselves and our journals, not for readers. They do not have to be understood at all. So we can make them quite subjective and use references that no one else might comprehend. Some of our poems not even we understand fully, as the poet Billy Collins smilingly says: "I took it as a good sign that I did not understand my poem."

A poem can certainly leave us with a sense of mystery, but it does not work well when it leaves us merely confused. If a poem requires the reader to work on discovering its meaning, it encourages careful focus, and that is a boon. But a poem that simply frustrates the reader is not likely to be reread. A poem that is not understandable to an intelligent reader is not coming through very well as a poem. An effective poem does not necessarily tell the reader all about the *who, what, why,* or *when,* but it does certainly provide reasonable clues; it gives us an introduction to itself within the poem itself. We learn how to read it by how it is written. A successful poem will be comprehensible to an intelligent reader—but not so obvious that he or she loses interest.

A poem should show rather than tell feelings. Work with images and feelings just as they appear to you, using the words that fit, simply and yet colorfully and expressively. Then surprises may result and you may find a new mirror of yourself.

William Stafford suggested, "Go as straight as possible to how it is ...." We might add, " ... to us." A poem does not have to present reality as it is by scientific measurement or definition, but as it appears to us and as it arouses our personal response. We go as straight as possible to how we are inside what is or how we are facing it or how it is facing us. In "The Noble Rider and the Sound of Words," Wallace Stevens said, "The subject matter of poetry is not that collection of solid, static objects extended in space but the life that is lived in the scene that it composes; and so reality is not that external scene but the life that is lived in it."

An experience can stand alone and be completed once it is over, like a tap on a drum. On the other hand, there can be implications in an experience that take time to reveal themselves, like the lingering resonance of a struck gong. Meaning co-arises between ourselves and the event. It may have one meaning today and another next week. For instance, a family photo may come to mean more now than it did thirty years ago. The *Mona Lisa* has meanings in our age that may be quite different from those of the past. To cherish or process an important event in our lives, we may write a poem about it. Perhaps we can try writing another poem on the same subject a month later, and yet another one a year later. Finely done is not always finally done.

The ripening power of time can be reflected in our poems, as it is in our conscious experience. To honor timing in that way is a fundamental orientation toward life that helps us respect the course of evolution beyond our control. We cannot adjust the hands of time, only say yes to the circle they continue to describe.

> Can I be expressive enough as a person that what I am will be communicated unambiguously?
>
> —CARL ROGERS

PRACTICE

Read all the instructions in the first paragraph first. Read the second paragraph only after you have completed the instructions in the first.

Close your eyes and explore your face with your dominant hand, as a blind person does. With your nondominant hand scribble words that describe your experience of your face. Do not think or plan, only write what comes to mind immediately no matter how far-fetched or incomprehensible. Then move to other parts of your body and do the same. After exploring each area, jot down your impressions on separate sheets of paper. Do this with your eyes remaining closed and still using your nondominant hand. You decide how clothed you want to be to perform this exercise. It is essential not to rush but to explore gently and firmly with your fingertips and then your palm. You do not have to include your whole body unless you want to. Any five areas of your body are enough.

Open your eyes and assemble the pages in any order. Using your dominant hand this time, write a poem that describes your favorite place in nature using only the words you have jotted down.

The Oomph of Images

There are rarely four successive lines in Shakespeare that do not include an image. This may account for some of the great power in his poetry. When we are given the opportunity to think in pictures, our imaginations are aroused and we are entertained.

Images roost in our minds, consciously or unconsciously, because they have something more to say than we have yet comprehended. In that sense, every image is transcendent, that is, spiritual. Poetry can be an opportunity to express the More. Any image that has captured our attention over the years—or just today—may likewise have a meaning that is ready to be revealed. Our dreams show that our souls are rich with images, even composed of them. We contact the depths of ourselves when we attend to images and work with them. Indeed, Aristotle said, "Image is the language of the soul."

Poetry, like dreams, presents images that visualize rather than ideas that conceptualize. This is why poetry is a language from and to the soul. Poetry can also be off-putting, because it arises from and looks into the unconscious. Yet, by using the practices in this book, we can become more adept at opening ourselves to the images, dreams, and poems that keep waiting to be delivered into consciousness. Reading and writing poetry are both midwifery, after all.

Images in our minds also turn us into visionaries. We meet up with the ordinary, pay attention to it mindfully, and then awake to it imaginatively. This can be a definition of poetry as well as our practice of it.

Hamlet, gazing at Yorick's skull, recalled Alexander the Great and the existential issue of our common human mortality. Thus, he moved from a personal event to an archetypal reality. His experience became more intense and certainly more insightful than before he had picked up the skull. Everything we meet in life is just such a skull. The more we look at it carefully and twirl it in our hands, the more we know ourselves and the larger world. Carl Jung wrote, "An image . . . usually will alter as the mere fact of contemplating it animates it. . . . Conscious and unconscious are united, in this way, as a waterfall connects above and below . . . . Creative ideas can appear that were never conscious before. They grow up from the dark depths like a lotus."*

We gaze at a religious icon so that we can become the figure it represents or enter the scene it depicts. We thereby interiorize spiritual identities, powers, and meanings. The same thing can happen with poems. Words and images become our shrines. Imagination is the gravitational field of the mind reaching into more elevated realms than the conceptual mind can guess are there. Poems, our own or those of others, are the eagles that fly us to those heights. The philosopher Ernst Cassirer wrote, "The poetic imagination is the only clue to reality."†

We see a painting of a ship in port. We are struck by the image and it remains in our minds. We pay attention to the scene it summons up in our imagination. This leads us to play with the image that has

---

* From *The Symbolic Life,* in *Collected Works,* volume 18 (Princeton: Princeton University Press, 1953–79), p. 37.

† From *An Essay on Man: An Introduction to a Philosophy of Human Culture* (New Haven, Conn.: Yale University Press, 1944).

fascinated us. We begin to see ourselves on the ship or as the ship. We allow the ship to speak to us—as in active imagination—and we are greeted with metaphors and surprising new images that spin off from the original one. We find resemblances in our own story, challenges and comforts too. The poem we then write will be rich and the ship in port will relay our personal experience to a reader. We ourselves will find depths of meaning that we would not have noticed before writing our poem. These meanings may reflect realizations of people who lived—and wrote—before us. This is why composing a poem is such an exhilarating form of creativity.

> A person is no longer a distinct individual, but his mind widens out and merges into the mind of mankind, not the conscious mind but the unconscious mind of mankind where we are all the same.
>
> —CARL JUNG

EXERCISES

Working with Images

Compose a poem that describes the picture you always drew in grammar school when your teacher asked the class to draw something. You are now simultaneously returning to childhood imagination and recalling an image that may have been waiting all this time to tell you something. For instance, maybe you always drew a red-winged blackbird perching in bulrushes. Draw this same picture now and notice how familiar it is to you. Speak to or become the bird and hear what it says back to you. Notice the bulrushes and let them have a say too. Notice the blank space around the scene and realize it is sky. Let it speak too. Do all this in writing. Then go back and omit the words and phrases that seem superfluous. Keep cutting down the stanzas to the basic points. Then arrange them in short lines and work with the rhythms in them so that they sound right to you. "Right" means they have a musical or pleasing flow. There is no right and wrong in this or any exercise in this book.

Your way is *the* way, since the goal is not to write great poems but to find great help for or make great discoveries about yourself in writing them.

———

Write out, in the form of a poem, the first dream you remember. Then stay with the central image of the dream until it changes of its own accord. Notice what it becomes, but don't force it in that direction. Put this too into poetic form. Carl Jung suggested that our first remembered dream forecasts the theme of our life. Has this been true for you?

Sharing Your Poems with Others

It's important to share what we write, not only with friends but with the outside world. This is how we move from individual work in the psychological realm to entering the empire of universal human connection, the spiritual universe. Here are some suggestions:

- Take a class on poetry writing or find a group of other poets with whom you can workshop your poems, that is, give feedback to one another about your work. This also gives you a chance to read your poems aloud. Poetry is not meant to languish on a page. It is the art of the spoken word. It is a dialogue between the poet and the listener. It is also useful to have everyone in the group write poems within ten minutes and then read them to one another. The short time allotment means less chance for revision and less self-consciousness, and that adds to the value—and the fun—of the experience.
- Attend poetry readings to hear poems more often and in new environments. This helps support other poets and encourages you to present your own poems to the public. In addition, visualization is a way of gaining more skill. The poets whom we see reading aloud are living visualizations of success in writing and presenting, and they therefore boost our belief in our own potential to do the same.

- Don't be hesitant about submitting your poems for publication. Show yourself that you have an interest in sharing what you write. This leads to more respect for your own work. The rejection letters, if there are any, cannot interfere with that joy. Most encouraging is the fact that you have asserted yourself in your own voice. To have expressed what is original rather than derivative is immensely rewarding, no matter whether you receive five A's for your work.

Emily Dickinson had the inner freedom to rethink everything for herself and so achieved a cognitive originality . . .

—HAROLD BLOOM

3

Healing the Past

What I have left behind has not left me.

—DAVID WHYTE

The first challenge in our present life is to be done with the past. Most of us enter adulthood bearing the wounds of childhood. These wounds take the form of instinctive needs unmet by our parents, specifically our needs for the five A's—attention, acceptance, appreciation, affection, and allowing. We may have been neglected or abandoned. We may have been abused or controlled. Our bodies have stored the memories of these losses and disappointments. They follow us through life in conscious and unconscious ways, influencing our choices in relationships. Our wounds from the past can vitiate our chances at happiness or love in our lives now. The healing work is to acknowledge our wounds and work through the memories and feelings that attach to them. The visualization that follows contributes to that project, the most poignant project in life, to grieve the holes in us and let go of blame toward those who drilled them.

The overall topic of this book is how psychological work and spiritual progress can happen through reading—and especially writing—poetry. There are depths in ourselves that may be unknown to us. They include unfinished business from our childhood, unexpressed and suppressed feelings, recognition of our own needs and wishes, and yearnings to fulfill our life purpose and gifts. When we read a poem by someone who has exhumed her own past or expressed her feelings, we may notice a similarity with our own. Then we find out what may have happened to us in our past or what we really feel now. The poem is a treasure map. When we write a poem about some life event we may notice that we are naming needs that we never guessed were in us or longings we were afraid to acknowledge. This is the power of poetry to grant us access to the lost or disavowed territories in ourselves. Poetry, of course, is totally legitimate when it is written or read just for fun or for an appreciation of language or images. But we would miss out on its many-splendored possibilities if we did not also reach into poetry to explore our buried treasures. Walt Whitman expressed the venture of self-discovery in his poem "In paths untrodden" (*Leaves of Grass,* 1900): "I know now a life, which does not exhibit itself . . . I celebrate that concealed but substantial life." Poetry reveals our unthought-of life.

Introduction to the Visualizations

The term *visualization* can refer to a kind of wordless imaging, but here it refers to a guided imagery that uses words. There are four visualizations scattered throughout the book. They follow four topics that we consciously explore: how our childhood influences our psychological work, how we open ourselves, how we say yes to what happens, and how we honor the seasons and transitions of life. The visualizations help us round out our conscious look at these areas by accessing our unconscious healing powers with respect to each of them. In addition, the visualizations serve to open and expand our imagination.

As a preparation for each visualization, you can lie or sit with your legs uncrossed, focusing on one sentence or paragraph at a time. Suggestions will be made to your inner mind that you may not notice consciously. It is not important or even necessary to analyze or concentrate too intensely. You can trust your inner self to take just what it needs and to discard the rest. The results can be trusted to happen at just the right time.

The visualization in this chapter, as well as the ones that appear throughout this book, are meant to be worked with more than once. You may notice that you focus on new areas each time. Remember that what is most important is your personal, unique response. As soon as you find the launching pad for inner work, follow your own imagination and feeling. Focus on opening that center within yourself where fears give way to love, where the intellect and ego give way to imagination, where self-blame becomes acceptance, where clinging becomes letting go.

The visualizations are intended to guide you in such a way that you not only imagine but *feel* the wholeness—both psychological and spiritual—that has always been within you. That wholeness may have felt fragmented over the years by self-doubt and fear.

The more we work on ourselves, the better we feel about ourselves. The more we acknowledge the broken pictures we have created, the more we see the intact reality of our inner self, beyond our pictures, poses, and postures. There is something wonderful in us and about us, as the Sufi poet Rumi says: "What God said to the rose to make it that beautiful, he has said to my heart one hundred times more."

Here are more specific ways to prepare for this and all the visualizations in this book:

- Scan your body for tension, passing from head to toe, and wherever you notice it, let it go. In this process stay with your breathing, bringing your breath to the tense places and thereby relaxing them. Take a deep breath and let it out, and as you do so, notice yourself becoming even more relaxed.

- Notice whether your mouth is closed tightly, and if it is, open your jaw slightly, sensing how this relaxes you even more. If your eyes are tightly closed, just let them be closed without holding them tightly shut. In every way you're letting go of the tensions you carry around with you in ordinary life. You are arriving at a space in which it is easy to feel calm—or rather, feel the calmness that has always been in you.

- Breathe slowly and regularly, notice each breath, in and out. Between each full breath, notice a space, a brief interval between your in-breath and your out-breath. Attend to these spaces so that the breaths become a background. Stay with the spaces between the breaths. Let yourself notice each gap and let yourself go, falling through one of these recurring gaps. Feel yourself passing through the spaces in your breath into no-where in particular.

Now begin the first visualization.

VISUALIZATION

Renewing Childhood

You let yourself go back in time and you stop whenever in your history you choose. It can be in early childhood, later childhood, adolescence, anytime before adulthood. You picture yourself now at the age you have settled on.

You see yourself at the kitchen or dining-room table of your house at that time. You look around and notice who's there. Everyone in your family!

Look at each of their faces. Is anyone looking at you? If so, do you notice any expression?

You're simply present. You're simply allowing yourself to be there in this reverie. Not requiring anything. Nothing to be said yet. Just a scene in your mind.

Looking around the table, your eye comes to rest on one of the people there: mother, father, brother, sister, whomever you choose.

And you're saying something, something about how you felt toward that person. You're simply allowing yourself to say something you always wanted to say but couldn't in the past because of embarrassment or shame or inhibition. Or maybe you just didn't know. But now you do know and are free to say what you know.

And whether or not that person heard you or paid attention to you in early life does not matter now, because now he or she turns to you with totally focused attention and listens to what you have to say.

You have a statement to make to him or her, and you are making it, and you are being heard and understood.

You go from person to person in your picture, making a statement to each one, and as you do so, each one turns and looks at you as if he or she had been waiting his whole life to hear this from you, really interested, really focused, really attentive, really letting you in.

No one is answering. This is how you want it to be. You want total listening without a response, a defense, an explanation, an excuse, a revision, a criticism, a denial.

And now you're aware that there are some things you would like to ask for. Again, you are not in need of a response, just experiencing the power of asking for what you want. You ask directly. The sky's the limit.

You notice what you ask for. You ask each person for something emotional, physical, spiritual, whatever you would like, no matter how embarrassing it may be, no matter how embarrassing it may have been. Now you are able to ask directly for what you've always wanted from that person, even if it's something that is out of character for him or her to give in real life.

Again you go from person to person, and each one turns with kindly and solicitous attention to you as you ask for what you want. Each person may give it or not, but each person listens and understands your need. You are satisfied either way.

Now you're aware you have some amends to make. You are aware that there are some ways you didn't come through for others. There may have been ways in which you hurt someone.

You go from person to person now, and to any one of them to whom you owe an amend, you make it. You admit some way in which you hurt, betrayed, or disappointed this person, and you ask for forgiveness.

And you assure each one, one at a time, that your commitment to integrity and loving-kindness, your new focus in life now, prevents you from doing anything hurtful again.

You are also aware of how some or all of the family have hurt you.

You ask each of them to make amends to you. Asking each one of whom it's appropriate for an admission that there was some way in which he or she hurt you, and an agreement that it won't happen again.

You can tell as you do this whether or not it's in character in real life for that person, but that does not matter now. You know this is empowering inner work, so each person is responding exactly as you want and making these amends.

And now you're aware of appreciation and gratitude. You go from person to person and express an appreciation or thanks for something about that person that you've noticed over the years, that you've loved, enjoyed, found helpful, and you express it openly to one person at a time.

This makes you feel lighter. You have a sense of a healing light that comes through you. This light beams through you to everyone in this room, the room in your mind, this kitchen where everyone is gathered now, as they were gathered so many times before.

You have a sense that you are beaming light to each of them, no matter where they are now, that they are receiving this light from you, whether in this world or from another.

You know there's something about this experience of asking for what you want, of appreciating, of thanking, of exchanging amends, of speaking up that brings light through you now in a spiritual way, to every one of them.

And with this sense of light that beams away bitterness and resentment, you now notice that each person beams light back to you. You are thankful.

Now you notice the door that leads out of the kitchen. Your eye is on that door now. You will be leaving this place with a sense of completion, with a sense of having taken care of something, with a sense that you can go freely, safely, lovingly, peacefully.

You're moving to that door now, and opening it. You're stepping outside, not taking anyone with you, because each has his own work to do. You are going to allow each one to do that work in his or her own way, to go through that door when each is ready.

But this is your turn, and you're going through. You're going with a sense of relief and release from any of the turmoil that may have happened there in childhood.

In fact, you are leaving childhood behind for now. You're going to the place in your heart that represents the freedom to be yourself, to experience your own wholeness.

You're stepping outside your history, to live in your own present, noticing how the light remains behind you as you walk through the door, how it goes on healing those inside, and how it precedes you as you enter the here-and-now space, bringing healing to those in your present world.

You see yourself standing alone, with a sense of power, a source of light, radiating loving-kindness. And you hear yourself repeating these affirmations:

I accept myself more and more.
I leave behind the baggage of the past.
I mend my antagonisms with people or circumstances.
I create new vistas for myself.
I am loved and appreciated by everyone who matters to me.
I have released the hurt that was within me.
I am here now in joy and peace.

Now there is something luminous in you, to you, and through you, and it shines from past to present to future.

Finally, you see yourself again at the age you originally chose. But there's something different about you now. You're clearer. You appreciate that you have released something. You look at your adult hands, and in your mind's eye place them, palms down, on the head of the figure of yourself from younger days. You now see beams of healing light passing through your hands into the head of your younger self. You step back and see your entire form as if illuminated, and then become one with it, with the healed child of the past, who is now free to emerge from inside you.

Now you are returning to this time and place, bringing your consciousness back from this guided faraway world, from this house in your mind, returning to the here and now, refreshed.

Be open now to writing a poem that may be inspired by what you have seen in your mind's eye. That eye is imagination and is a midwife to your creativity. If you would like help in writing your poem, use any sentence or phrase in the visualization as the first line of your poem. Then let your imagination flow with any associations that follow. Do this spontaneously, in a free-flow, with no attempt to make your poem perfect. You can revise it later, but for now simply write out what your heart suggests to you.

EXERCISE

Journaling in Poetry

We should not be surprised if poetry opens a Pandora's box. Writing poems about life events, especially those of childhood, might release heretofore hidden and disturbing memories. Some of what happened to us has remained repressed for the sake of our own protection. We might not be ready to face certain facts about our history, so our unconscious keeps them safely buried. Such defenses are not necessarily pathological. They may simply be adaptive, honoring our timing. There is a time to know what happened, and sometimes it is best not to know at all. Nonetheless, our poetry can be the path to self-knowledge, a useful step toward self-liberation once the time is right for us. No more hiding is needed when we enter the world of free-speech poems that we write only for ourselves.

Keep a private journal in which you jot down words, thoughts, images, feelings, or moods that may propel you toward composing a poem. We may lose the building blocks of a poem if we do not have a way of keeping track of what has excited us in any particular moment. The words or images that strike us are examples of synchronicity, meaningful correspondences between what catches our attention and what we may be ready to explore.

Write in your journal about significant personal events or dreams, not in paragraph form but in lines, as if they were poems. This method starts journal entries off on the right footing, and you can later work with the ones that appeal to you to make them into more finished poems. Journal writing can make us long-winded and may diffuse or dull our energy. Poetic lines focus us and thereby deepen and sharpen our words.

As an alternative, write your journey entries in prose and when certain passages strike you as particularly moving or memorable, rewrite them in rhythmic lines and then work with the lines to shape them into a poem, revising over and over until you achieve the economy and diction you are seeking. And yes, some poems flow out perfectly and need no revision at all!

Here is an example of what seems to be a journal entry that easily became a poem for Walt Whitman ("O you whom I often and silently come" in *Leaves of Grass,* 1900). Notice that the poet is sharing something personal in each line. In the first two lines he reminds himself of how he acts toward a special someone. In the final line he describes—discovers—the taut and passionate feeling he has carried silently within himself. This poem puts the feeling into words so that it can be witnessed by the poet and later by readers. The identity of the other person is not revealed, but the poet has revealed his own longings in plain language. He is also working on himself in that he is processing his feelings, finding out more about what is happening within himself. This is how poetry journaling lends itself to becoming a more conscious path to the way we see ourselves.

> O you whom I often and silently come where you are, that I
> may be with you;
> As I walk by your side, or sit near, or remain in the same room
> with you,
> Little you know the subtle electric fire that for your sake is
> playing within me.

In his book *True Perception: The Path of Dharma Art,* the Tibetan meditation master Chögyam Trungpa writes, "We could almost say that being willing to be a fool is one of the first wisdoms." Let go of having to make sure that what you write in your journal sounds good, logical, polite, wise, correct, or proper. Those considerations have no place in writing poetry. They hearken from inhibitions imposed by the critical voices that prevent your full emergence, which is the very purpose behind your expressing your poetic voice.

In your journal, ask yourself what of you was ignored, shut off, slammed shut? What is hidden in your persona, your social mask? Let that out in an unconventional, unobstructed way, even if it is obscene, pornographic, taboo, irreverent, blasphemous, awkward, or untidy. Write out your most embarrassing desires, darkest fears, cruelest intentions. Ordinary speech can be carefully designed to maintain politeness. Our poetic voice is free of that limitation.

Let your poetry be an exodus from restriction. Let your poetry be your chance at freedom of self-expression. Let your poetry be the breakthrough of your own voice and truth into the world. Use your writing to follow what Norman Mailer calls "that uncharted journey into the rebellious imperatives of the self." The language of that rebellious self is such a wonderful tool in the composing of your poem.

Any subject is worthy of a poem. It does not have to be exalted, any more than we have to be. The poet Louise Glück wrote, "It was clear to me long ago that any hope I had of writing real poetry depended on my living through common experiences. The privileged, the too-protected, the mandarin in my nature would have to be checked."

Writing a poem can be like the practice that Carl Jung suggested we employ to work on our dreams, "active imagination." This is done by opening a dialogue with your dream characters:

Record your dreams in your poetry journal. Then ask what they have come to tell you. Play the part of each person, place, or thing in the dream and hear what they and you spontaneously declare. Dialogue back and forth in writing, using short lines rather than paragraphs. A poem can develop as the result of that work. You are linking unconscious images with conscious realizations, meeting what arises from your hidden inner depths with your own immediate wording.

I recently dreamed of my mother gently and tenderly holding me and my asking her about her relationship with my dad. It was a very warm and safe moment between us, one that has not actually happened in our life together so far. When I awoke, I did not recall what she said in the dream in answer to my question. That morning I wrote what my mother might have said. The poem that resulted proved to be an unusually revealing pathway into understanding my parents' relationship—as well as what I have sought in my own relationships.

The poetic mind that clicks in when we place the intention of writing a poem arouses our unconscious. Then we access meanings hitherto unknown to us. Our dreams show that something is ready to be opened, and our poems open it.

ADDITIONAL EXERCISES FOR USING POETRY TO HEAL THE PAST

A poem of "found language" is one that arises from what we hear or read. As an exercise, we can notice statements in conversations or in films that strike us as memorable or playful. We might also notice something we hear or read as somehow more meaningful than we can yet appreciate. We can use these statements as the framework of a poem.

We find some things *touching* and that means *inspiring*. Some of the words we recall as touching in our past, especially within our family or in an intimate relationship, may already be poetry. Our challenge is simply to recall and write. Consider the first example poem in the appendix. It is based on a conversation with my mother about a dialogue she had with my grandmother regarding the deaths of her two sons, my uncles. Notice the unusual diction as I attempt to reproduce the Italian-American colloquialisms. In your poem of such "found conversation," include the natural speech patterns of the person you are quoting.

Healing is not caused by us; it happens to us. This is called grace. Make a list of the many graces you may now remember as you look back over your life. Add specifically applicable words of thanks to each listing. You may also notice where you feel the graces and the thanks in your body. This may happen automatically or by dancing or moving in some rhythmic way that enacts your sense of grace or expresses your thanks. Let words come and voice them. They are your poems.

The Making of a Healing Poem, Step-by-Step

Here is an opportunity to watch a poem emerge step-by-step. I present four versions of a poem of mine and explain each of my revisions. In addition, I end this section with a detailed explanation of how the writing of the poem seemed to contribute to some psychological and spiritual progress. Between versions, by the way, I made minor changes, which I do not show here. There may actually have been ten to fifteen versions in all. Version 4 may not be final, since I may come back to this poem in the months to come.

After watching the Western *Shane* for the fourth time, I noticed I still felt so touched by the ending. The story is about a family—father, mother, young son—who are visited by a gunfighter, Shane, who successfully helps them defend their ranch and then is wounded, perhaps fatally, and rides off alone into the sunset. The son, Joey, has related to Shane as a father figure. He fervently calls after him not to go, but Shane keeps riding away without answering or turning around.

This time, as I watched the ending with my usual tears, but with stronger than usual emotions, I made the connection between Shane leaving Joey and my own father leaving me and Mom when I was two. I wondered if I cried after him as Joey did. I wrote all this in my journal. In the process, I noticed how I also feel grief in my present life when men who have become father figures vanish from my life by death or choice.

What I am describing is an area of my own life that is still not fully resolved. My grief about the loss of Dad and my consequent transference of father energy onto others give me clues that I still have much to process from my childhood. The poem that follows is an example of how poetry writing can be a way of doing some of this psychological work.

When I feel something strongly, I know it is a poem in the making, so I went to work, using what for me is the simplest way to write a poem. I first gave myself permission to write my ideas and feelings *any old way*—no attempt to be grammatical, use proper English, be logical, create a masterpiece. What follows in this first version is what I came up with as *I wrote with no stops or revisions. I thought in prose statements but arranged them on the page as a poem.* Using that style shifts me into a poetic mood and that is why I highly recommend it. The words flowed out naturally, since I had given up

having to pay careful attention to poetic diction. I noticed I nonetheless became somewhat lyrical in my writing of the last line.
The title is *Watching Shane.*

Version 1:

It never fails that
I feel with the boy Joey
As he is crying out after the disappearing Shane.

Though mother is at home for me,
We are both saying:
"Come back. We need you."
Maybe those were the very words
That were said inside my little body
When Dad rode off
Long ago.
Maybe that explains
How I become so attached and feel so bad
When father figures now
Disappear into the sunset.

For version 2, I changed the first stanza by speaking directly to
Joey. I felt that this style of a dialogue with someone who felt what
I felt made my poem more powerful. In the second line, I described
Joey's body language and added more about Shane's lack of response. I placed the name "Shane" on a new line to emphasize his
solitary style and to dramatize his separation from Joey. This seemed
to set the scene more poignantly, as the film did too.

In the second stanza I shortened the introduction to the mother
figure and made Joey's plea and mine into one. The quotation from
the film is exact, so it does not change.

In the third stanza, I omitted *little body,* as it sounded like self-pity.
I used more economy so that I could make the point without so
many unnecessary words. I added the word *keening,* which refers
to grief, and *shrill* to refer to how loud my cry must have been in
the echo chamber of my body in childhood, though not expressed

in words as it is now. I added *so* to *long ago* to play on the words *so long* for "goodbye." I wanted to find little ways to keep this poem from being too serious. At the same time, a serious *intention* rescues a poem from becoming a mere playing with words.

In the fourth stanza, I again trimmed words and this led me to a colorful image, *spur into me,* which fits the Western theme, as do the words *cowpokes* and *rode off* (though Dad used a car, not a horse). By adding *gut* I made it more physical and masculine. I used the name "Joey" to show I was still addressing him. I changed *sunset* to *dusk* to create alliteration with the word *disappear.* Both words say the same thing, but one more appropriately fits the fading quality of the ending of the film and of relationships that end mysteriously.

Version 2:

> Every time I am feeling it all with you, Joey,
> So all-arched toward
> The vanishing—
> And unanswering—
> Shane:
> Mother at home and one lone plea:
> "Come back. We need you."
> Perhaps those very words
> Were keening shrill in me
> When Dad rode off,
> So long ago.
>
> How those yearnings even now
> Spur into me, gut-deep, Joey,
> When cowpokes get to mean so much,
> And disappear into the dusk.

In version 3, I changed the first stanza by using *This time too,* which seems better by its colloquialism than what I had before. With the words *too* and *you* I was able to use internal rhyme (rhyme within a single line). I changed *all-arched* to *ache-arched* to show the grief dimension early on in the poem and to use a phrase that might catch the reader's attention by its unusual combination of words. It is also alliterative, which adds to the lyricism I wanted to achieve.

In the second stanza, I omitted the reference to "mother" because it did not seem appropriate to include her without more explanation. Such an explanation would have dulled the impact of the true focus of the poem: a boy and a dad. Also, I made the pitiable cry of Joey, and me, more stark by having it sit out there as its own stanza.

I changed the third stanza to a question in order to make more contact with the reader. I am asking Joey, but I am asking the reader too. I changed *so long ago,* which is a cliché to *way back then,* which is colloquial and more like what a Westerner might say. Also, I now used iambic pentameter in how I designed the word arrangement in the first three lines of the stanza. This adds to the sonority, though it also shows—for better or worse—that I am still tied to that tradition.

In the fourth stanza, I added *ever-ancient new* to the first line to pose an existential question within the poem. This was meant to elicit a more universal appeal. For this same reason, I omitted Joey's name and thereby addressed the reader. I added *very, very* to show how serious my need for substitutes can be. I was now caught by iambic rhythm and could not resist using it all the way. I added *muted* because it fit Shane's—and Dad's—lack of responsiveness as they rode off, and it fit the time of day, since "muting" is what light is doing in the sunset. Also, *muted* was alliterative with *mean* and *much.* The final alliteration is *disappear* and *dusk.*

Version 3

> This time too, I am feeling it all with you, Joey,
> So ache-arched toward
> The vanishing—
> And unanswering—
> Shane:
> "Come back. We need you."
> Were those the very words
> That keened so shrill in me

When Dad rode off for good,
Way back then?

The yearning ever-ancient new
Spurs into me, gut-deep,
When cowpokes come to mean so very, very much,
And disappear into the muted dusk.

For version 4, I changed the first line to make it crisper and kept
the rest of the stanza almost the same. I took out the extra *And* before *unanswering* for more directness. I omitted the colon at the end
to leave space, which fits the space or gap that Shane's vanishing
creates for Joey—and me.

In the second stanza I added exclamation points, to show the emphasis both Joey and I placed on the plea.

I changed the last line of stanza three from *Way back then,* which
denotes only time, to *With no goodbye or why.* The original line seemed
wasted when it referred only to how long ago Dad left. The new line
adds poignancy by showing the suddenness, incompleteness, and confusion that characterized the event. Also, I am playing on the word *good*
in the line above. I omitted the comma at the end of the line since it
seems unnecessary and breaks the breathlessness I want to achieve. In
addition, I have used an internal rhyme, *bye* and *why.* For alliteration, I
begin and end the line with a *w,* which also begins the line above.

I added the word *still* in the fourth stanza to connect it to the
third stanza about Dad. The fourth stanza omits *ever* before *ancient,*
since the phrase seems old-fashioned or religious, which is not in
keeping with the theme. By keeping the word *ancient* I allude to
the archetypal experience of all children whose dads disappeared.
I changed the first line completely, believing that the new version
more clearly makes my point about similar characters I myself meet.
I changed *into* to *in* to show the depth of the wound rather than the
piercing action of it. This change also honors the iambic rhythm in
the stanza. I made *gut-deep* a new line to emphasize the sharpness
of my feeling. I rearranged the last two lines to make them three so
that the reader can slow down and really absorb the final words and

sentiments. I omitted *very, very* as too dramatic and petulant, which contradicts the restraint I am going for. I made the *disappear* more stark by putting it on a separate line. I notice again and like that *disappear* and *dusk* both begin with the same letter. This alliteration links the concepts they represent and makes them evocative of the feelings they imply. I changed *and* to *but* for emphasis and clarity, though I am still not sure if that is a good revision.

I noticed that in this overall revision I was making far fewer changes than usual. This led me to believe that the poem could now stand as it was. Also, I became less interested in it. I no longer felt the animation that moved me so passionately when I wrote the first versions. To me, that is the time to leave off writing and revising. New changes now could be anticlimactic and I could lose the spontaneity of my poem. Finally, in printing this poem, I can use a font to fit the Western flavor such as "Chalkboard."

In this final version, I noticed for the first time, without having planned it, that the poem is about the film in the first stanza, about me in the second, and about me and everyone in the third stanza. I like that progression. Also, the ending opens a topic and thereby leaves the reader with a new subject to ponder.

Final version:

This time too, I'm with you, Joey,
So ache-arched toward
The vanishing—
Unanswering—
Shane

"Come back! We need you!"
Were those the very words
That keened so shrill in me
When Dad rode off for good
With no goodbye or why?

That ancient woe
Spurs in me still,

Gut-deep,
When cowpokes come to mean so much
But disappear
Into the muted dusk.

The title of a poem works best when it impacts the reader differently before and after reading the poem. Thus, before reading the poem, the title "Watching *Shane*" refers to watching a movie. After reading the poem, the title has expanded in meaning so that it now refers to pondering the person of Shane and his duplications as my own Dad and then as other father figures. A title introduces a poem and hopefully creates an interest in the reader. When the reader looks back at the title, he or she sees more, and that is satisfying, a purpose of poetry to be sure.

We shape poetry as we shape pottery, continually re-forming until what we see fits what we want to create. We are not simply reworking words when we keep revising. William Butler Yeats, commenting on revising his poetry, said, "It is myself that I remake." We are redefining ourselves, not just the phrases that make up our poems. *My work on my poem was work on myself.* This is how writing a poem is a tool for self-discovery that does so much more than mere thinking about ourselves.

A poem can spring from any origin, and its motivation does not have to be fully understood. Composing this poem helped me work through some of my childhood issues, especially grief. I did not begin with that motivation but received that benefit as a resultant gift. (This for me was an example of life's synchronicity: I wrote the poem while finishing my book *When the Past Is Present: Healing the Emotional Wounds That Sabotage Our Relationships.*)

Healing our emotional wounds is a process that involves four basic steps:

1. We *address* our concerns rather than deny them, distract ourselves from them, or run from them.

2. We *process* our issues by experiencing the full range of feelings they arouse, without inhibition or blame of others but as our own responsibility. In addition, we look for ways the present event that is

stressing us hooks up to our past and may be gathering energy from transference onto the present.

3. This makes us ready to *resolve* our issue by letting go of it and/ or by making a commitment to ourselves, or to someone else, to change something in our behavior. This is how we break out of our negative patterns.

4. Finally, we *integrate* our new realizations and commitment into how we live our lives. We implement our resolve; we make it part of how we behave from now on.

The refining of my poem led me to more depth in all four areas: *addressing* my father issue and my transferences, *processing* my own loss and disappointment, *resolving* the issue by letting go, and *integrating* what I learned about myself into how I will interact with future father figures. Before writing, I transferred my father issues and needs onto others unconsciously; now I can be more alert about what I am doing. I can take my admiration or attachment as a pointer to my own grief regarding my own father. Then I can more easily reduce the new father figures to ordinary size in my mind rather than making them so important. The work is one of both feeling feelings and revising thoughts.

In addition, after writing the poem and recalling that Shane was wounded when he left Joey, I realized that my dad, too, was wounded by his own life experience, so his leaving was not really about me. This led to more compassion for him. I see that shift in myself as an example of how psychological work can lead to spiritual practice. This is an example of how we combine steps we take with shifts that happen, a process that occurs both in our psychological work and in our spiritual practice.

It was a spiritual practice to put this poem together, because I began in mindfulness and moved through imagination into loving-kindness—the model we are using throughout this book. Here is how it happened: First, I found myself looking at my life experience *mindfully*—without judgment—and this opened me to a tender sorrow for all the players in my story, Mom, Dad, and me. My *imagination* led me to see the connection between Dad and Shane and father figures, as well as between Joey and me. Imagination also gave me words and images with which to tell my story. In addition, I seemed to be making contact with children everywhere who experience loss in the same primal way that it happened to me. I saw Joey as the archetype of that poignant theme. In that sense, I became conscious collectively, not only personally. This led me to compassion and to the practice of *loving-kindness:* wishing happiness and resolution for all families who live with loss and for all fathers who are absent in some way. In any case, simply writing a poem is enough for a psychological and spiritual experience, even without the specific steps and shifts that happened for me. Our unconscious is animated by our poems, without our noticing.

Here is one more way the psychological and spiritual unite: the psychological work of resolving an issue produces a spiritual result. The restless ego mind thrives on obsessing, rerunning the old tapes about what happened in the past and who may be to blame. For instance, the ego may hold on to a grudge. To resolve such a mind-set is to let it go, usually by forgiveness. This releases the clutch of the chronically jammed mind and invites it to open into a new spaciousness, finally free of its stuckness. To remain attached to an issue or story is how our ego interrupts our journey to spiritual awareness. To resolve and let go is how we become free to enjoy our full spiritual consciousness. This is an example of how our psychological work leads to a spiritual gain.

I worked on this poem seriously every day for ten days. Now I can show it to some of my poetry friends and ask for their feedback, which may lead to new changes. I gain a lot from feedback, questions, and even criticisms. But a poem is like a signature, too—beyond final verdicts from outside.

My own critique of my poem is that it may be too short. All the information in the opening paragraphs of this section is missing. Yet this poem is meant to be personal to me and for my own growth in consciousness of who I am, so I am not so concerned about that.

I realize also that I am risking not gaining a wider audience by making the seeing of the film so crucial to my poem. The poem may not make sense to those who have not seen it. But I wrote from personal motivation, so that does not matter. Also, the film has become a classic and can easily be found in libraries. It is even described online in a number of sites.

I am also very aware that this poem, and all my poems in this book, do not qualify as great poetry, but I am hoping that they encourage my readers not to wait to be perfect poets either. Sincere willingness to learn and to experiment is all that counts.

I found myself extremely focused on this poem, and that excited me and kept me working. Focus and excitement are the equivalent of inspiration. I certainly felt that the poem was somehow writing itself at the beginning and that my task was to welcome it, that is, to let it awaken and stretch more fully into itself. Perhaps, at the best, this is what our parents are meant to do for us, welcome us at birth and then stay long enough to help us develop into who we really are. We can compose poems that honor that if it happened, and help us make peace with it if it did not.

The past buries the past and must end in silence, but it can be a conscious silence that rests open-eyed. Perhaps this is the final forgiveness . . .

—IRIS MURDOCH, *The Sea, the Sea*

4

Learning to Let Go

To be a discoverer you hold close whatever you find and
after awhile you decide what it is and then, secure in where
you have been, you turn to the open sea and let go.

—WILLIAM STAFFORD

The little birds in the nest have to let go of the
warmth of their mother's breast if they are ever to fly. Our human
life is a series of such letting-go experiences so that we can take
hold of what comes next in life. Since our longing is to go on a
journey, like the birds, letting go of comfort and stability is necessary as we face each new threshold on the path. Once over a threshold, all is reversed and we take hold again before the next letting
go. We let go of comforts in order to face challenges; we let go of
challenges in order to enjoy comforts. We let go of rigid beliefs in
order to open our imagination; we let go of constant investigation
in order to commit to a belief. We let go of our ego-centeredness in
order to enter into an intimate relationship; sometimes we have to
let go of a relationship in order to find ourselves again.

Poetry is certainly a practice of letting go. In the writing of a
poem, we let go of our logical and rational mind-sets in order to
cross the threshold into freewheeling creativity. In reading poems,
we let go of our analytic style of thinking in favor of a synthetic
sense of what the poet is revealing. We let go of our need to understand it all in favor of honoring a mystery.

We also want to find out what our own inner self wants to reveal
to us in the midst of the clatter of the world. This takes letting go
of our manic lifestyle long enough to pause and be silent so that

we can hear the chords of our own being above the cacophony of our distracting and seductive world. We let go of our firm grip of control on people and things so that our bodies and minds become geared to let in with courage rather than keep out with fear. Visualizations can help us let go long enough to find ourselves. The one that follows may be a useful tool in that project.

VISUALIZATION

Opening Ourselves

This visualization prepares you for the writing of a poem on the theme of letting go. If it helps, use chapter 3 as preparatory information for this as well as all the visualizations that follow.

You trust your body automatically to bring in what you need and to let go of what you do not need, and you're trusting that your psyche does the same thing.

You are letting go of what you no longer need, through every cell of your body, even though there's something within you that says, "I've got to hold on to this for dear life."

Now you're trusting what may happen in this exercise. You're looking back at some of the things in life that you've lost, that you've had to let go of, and you're allowing, in this moment, that it all be all right.

You know life can't be just breathing in, just collecting and holding on. It has to include the out-breath, the letting go.

You're aware, with thanks, of the things that have come to you, of the wonderful gifts that have been given to you, gifts that have arisen from within your own body, your enthusiasms, your intuitions, your feelings.

You are aware, with thanks, of the gifts that have come through relationships, through family life, through friends, through careers, all that you've appreciated and enjoyed, the things you have let in and still keep.

You also have let things go. And all of this now feels equal on your journey. Holding on or letting go, moving on or staying still. All of this is the same, just one full breath of life, both in and out.

You picture yourself now sitting by a waterfall. You see the water cascading in the sunlight. It continually lets go of any single position. It's allowing itself to fall through the air with no support, and to splash into the pool below, then into rivulets, into streams, and ultimately back to the ocean. You're looking in wonder at this cascade.

You love the ease with which the water allows itself to go, allows itself to fall. You can understand the word *fall*, the utter letting go, making no attempt to stop itself, the letting go that creates power. The power of the waterfall is in the falling.

You say, "My power is in the letting go of my usual position. My power is in dropping through the air, and as I let go, I find more power. As the water lets go, it creates power. As I let go, I create power for myself, the power to move on to what comes next in my life."

Now you see yourself sitting or standing, dancing, drinking, splashing, under the waterfall. You are allowing yourself to get wet. Doing what you want to do to be part of the scene, to let water happen to you. You're standing by, under, or within this waterfall.

You hear yourself singing to the waters:

"Because you've let go, I can receive you. Because you didn't hold on, a gift has been given to me. Because you didn't hold back, I have received something that helps me live, these purifying falls, these waters of rebirth."

And you're saying to yourself:

When I let go, I let myself live. When I don't hold back, I receive a gift and give one too. When I let myself fall, when I give up my ego's stubborn position, my rigidity, I find something new in life. I keep allowing this to happen.

I'm through with holding back. I'm through with having to maintain a fixed image of myself. I'm through with having to be right. I'm through with having to be justified or vindicated. I'm through with having to be sure I act as others expect.

Now I have no one left to blame, no one left to be better than, no one left that has to validate me, no one left that has to prop me up. I'm letting go of all that, trusting as the water does.

If I fall, I live, I go on. If I hold back, I stagnate. I choose life. I feel myself more and more in contact with a source of living water inside me. It rises like a spring and falls like a waterfall. It's happening inside me now and I trust it.

There will always be a spring of water rising and there will always be a falling of water, just as there will always be a spring season and a fall season. I allow this. I love this.

This is my power, my inner spring and my inner fall, all OK within me, I trust they will always be there, or rather here, already here now.

I thank the waterfall for all it has taught me today.

Now you are returning to this time and place, bringing your consciousness back from this guided world, from this contemplation, returning to the here and now, fully refreshed. Write a poem in your journal that flows from your experience in this visualization. Let it flow spontaneously with no attempt to revise or correct it.

To Think or to Imagine

The poet John Keats wrote, "I am certain of nothing but the holiness of the heart's affections and the truth of the imagination." Imagination is true to life, the life of infinite possibility in us. Indeed, imagination is a magnetic field drawing new possibilities to ourselves once our tender-footed egos are ready for visitation. Imaging, or visualization, is used in sports and in other areas to promote victory or success. As we increase our capacity to produce images by a liberated imagination, we actually further our own personal evolution.

Imagination also plays a part in how the world can change for the better. We can imagine peace and justice, not only work for it. We often underestimate the power of the mind to place and fulfill a grand intention. J. K. Rowling, author of the Harry Potter books, speaking to the graduating senior class at Harvard in 2008, said, "We do not need magic to change the world; we carry all the power we need inside ourselves already. We can *imagine* better."

Poetry arises from imagination easily when spontaneous experience is met with personal feeling. A feeling wants to find a manner of expression that suits the experience. So the poet marshals imagination and directs her feeling into words and figures of speech. The result is a pleasurable, affecting, and meaningful poem.

The philosopher René Descartes presented the premise "I think therefore I am." Indeed, Western philosophy focuses on the mind that can remain independent of the external world. When we are tied to such radical dualism, poetry becomes almost impossible, though standard science certainly flourishes. Perceptual knowledge places us firmly in a living experience. This is the garden in which poetry blooms. Abstract knowledge, on the other hand, works with concepts where intellect thrives.

In the nondual view, there is no sharp division between us in here and that out there. Buddhism especially denies the existence of a separate, independent, fixed self. It focuses on awareness of reality in the moment, and teaches that our mind and its concepts cannot exist independently of the world from which they arose and to which they return. In fact, in Buddhism all existence happens by contact *between* mind and world. Poetry happens precisely, and oh so colorfully, in that in-between space.

William Wordsworth spoke of "the meddling intellect." We may be suffering from an inhibited imagination or a lazy one, which is often the result of tightly held biases or fears of self-expansion. When what e. e. cummings called "the tall policeman of our mind" no longer oversees our thoughts, we have taken a step toward releasing our imagination. We can move in that direction by learning how to allow our imagination free rein and become open to whatever may arise. This is the opposite of policing, and we may thereby chance upon infinite possibilities in any reality or image. Reality, and our imagination riding upright on its back, can then run freely in any direction rather than be stuck in the corral of our reining definitions. Then we are free of what William Blake called our "mind-forged manacles."

If we believe that freedom of imagination is dangerous or sinful, we might engage in constant custody battles over our thoughts. It will be hard for the muse of poetry to visit us in such a maximum-security prison. The monitoring action of our rational mind—or scrupulous conscience—undercuts our imagination and prevents us from seeing ordinary things in new ways. As a result, we see an apple as an apple instead of as a globe. In his journal for 1840, Ralph Waldo Emerson shares a dream: "I dreamed that I floated at will in the great Ether, and I saw this world floating also not far off, but diminished to the size of an apple. Then an angel took it in his hand and brought it to me and said: 'This must thou eat.' And I ate the world."

The nonnegotiable accuracy of dictionary definitions robs reality of its mystery element. A grasp of reality is not simply seeing things denotatively—apples as fruit. It is seeing the connotations, the implicit, personal, and impressionistic meanings that imagination fosters—apple as Edenic, apple as cosmic, apple as everything. We then visit uncommon territories, the ones our linear minds cannot enter or even believe can exist, a parallel world within and around us.

It requires a poetic imagination to look under the given meanings of words and notice the vast spectrum of reality behind them. Our challenge is to widen and lengthen ourselves to accommodate the full range of implications in the words that appear in poems. As soon as any art is fully defined, it ceases to be art, since it is no longer alive. Meaningful poetry is like a cathedral, fully standing but never fully finished, or like a child, fully alive but ever growing.

When we live in our heads and keep ourselves safe from letting our minds wander, we are not in the best position for a journey, which is our central archetype and our uniquely human way of finding fulfillment. We miss the surprising glories and dangers that peep out at us everywhere, what Wallace Stevens calls "the essential poem at the heart of things." This takes trust in and intuition about surprising meanings and an imagination to see them.

Indeed, emancipated imagination is hospitable to the whole panoply of reality. We are open to the explicit and the implicit, the phenomenal world and the worlds beyond phenomenality, the light behind the darkness, the unrestricted behind the predetermined, the immortal beyond the momentary. The words *behind* and *beyond*, of course, always mean "permeating." To reach behind appearances is to notice the light coming through them.

A free imagination may offend some people, as our own freedom of choice does sometimes. It is up to us to maintain our courage in those moments. In the 1950s Allen Ginsberg wrote the poem "Howl," a very unconventional poem that was seen by some as obscene (in fact his publisher was arrested on obscenity charges). Ginsberg's comments on writing "Howl" are quite striking:

> I thought I would not write a poem but just write what I wanted to without fear, let my imagination go, open secrecy, and scribble magic lines from my real mind—sum up my life—something I wouldn't be able to show anybody, writ for my own soul's ear .... Have I really been attacked for this sort of joy?*

The judge who presided over the 1957 obscenity case, Clayton W. Horn, ruled that "Howl" was not obscene. In his ruling he made remarks that were equally stirring:

> Life is not encased in one formula whereby everyone acts the same or conforms to a particular pattern. No two persons think alike; we were all made from the same mold but in different patterns. Would there be any freedom of press or speech if one must reduce his vocabulary to vapid innocuous euphemism?†

Imagination and Personal Expansion

Rainer Maria Rilke wrote, "I want to unfold. I do not want to remain folded up anywhere, because wherever I am still folded, I am untrue." Openness of imagination requires a commitment to release

---

* Ginsberg, Allen. "Notes Written on Finally Recording *Howl*" in *Evergreen Review* 3, no. 10 (1959): 132–35.
† From *Howl on Trial: The Battle for Free Expression,* eds. Bill Morgan and Nancy Joyce Peters (San Francisco: City Lights Books, 2006).

ourselves from imprisonment in our own folded-up fixations, self-deceptions, divisions, biases. In the Buddhist perspective, openness reflects a marvelously abundant space called *shunyata,* "emptiness." To be "empty" means to be free of concepts, when everything can be spaciously and continuously unfolding, like morning glories in the sunlight. As we embrace shunyata, we discover a fullness and an openness to the infinite potential in ourselves and in our fuller being, all reality.

From this open and spacious standpoint, we marshal three responses in the face of any predicament: attentiveness, resilience, and stability. We *attend* to what is happening, noticing what we feel with no attempt to judge it. We are *resilient* as we roll with the punches, adjust to the circumstances, and deal with the chips wherever they have fallen. We are *stable* when a blow has fallen on us because we can feel it fully but it cannot stop or drive us. These three practices tap into our innate wisdom and sanity. We then act not out of habit but with creative imagination, released from its usual contractions. This is how we *tend* our experience rather than simply have it happen to us.

There is then no further need for possessiveness or aggressiveness. We feel ourselves free to be utterly defenseless and invincible at the same time. *Our vision of truth has become not definitive but evocative.* We then revert to our original nature: blissful, conscious, and unconditionally open. This establishes us in a new and true relationship to reality.

Awareness and concentration combine in poetry writing and reading, enabling us to focus in a way that makes us open to anything. We become permeable, letting the light through.

If we have been brought up in a conventional or rigid way, it may have hobbled our imagination, which is an insidious danger in any fundamentalist view of the world. Poetry permits us the heretical, unofficial, irreverent, uncertain version of experience. It is the only version that sets us free from encapsulation in the standard orthodox structures where we may find shelter but not ecstasy. Imagination allows us to stand outside, which is precisely what the word *ecstasy* means. In that eccentric space we contact our creative life, the other half of ourselves, the half that can, sadly, be so easily mislaid in the church of final truths.

As we free our imaginations, we more courageously allow the chaos or demons in ourselves to emerge. We learn to live with them, to hear from them, to receive their slanted blessings. We can live with questions and even be stirred by letting them remain questions. We do not have to visit the answer man in our minds so often. We welcome inscrutability and the unlighted side of life, givens of the, ah, sweet mystery of life.

As we have been seeing, our universal human challenge is to embark upon a heroic journey. Since this is what is required for us to evolve, an initial step of setting forth is primary. The freedom to move in our own direction is thus not a privilege but a requisite of growth. To go does not mean that we have to travel to Timbuktu. Going can be about breaking away from suffocating habits and attitudes. One way this can happen is by unshackling our imagination from its accustomed confines and its cramped expression. What follows are some suggestions that may help us open our imagination, another pathway to becoming ourselves unreservedly.

We affirm at the outset that our goal is not to put a stop to our logical thinking. We are often required to engage in focused thinking, concentrating on something that occupies us. We distinguish that intelligent use of our minds from the ongoing chatter in our heads, most of which we hardly notice. In imagination, however, the chatter becomes a useful launching pad for creativity.

EXERCISES

Unfolding Your Imagination

We can always stretch to be more than we are. For instance, try this simple exercise. Right now, take the deepest breath you can take and hold it. Now add just a little more of an inhale. Finally, add one more little inhale. Now breathe it all out. Notice that you took "the deepest breath" first, but with a little coaxing, you went further.

It is just like that in everything about us. We presume we know where the limit of our capacities and gifts may be. But with encouragement we can stretch, and then we realize we had more capacities and gifts than we thought. Our fixed beliefs and stunted imagination about life and ourselves are what limit us.

The four visualizations in this book are central to the widening of imagination. In addition, we can benefit from the practices that follow. Below is a list of ideas for short stories or poems. Choose one and in your writing use fanciful images that exaggerate the ideas. Begin each story or poem by brainstorming rather than narrowly focusing. Allow a free-floating, spontaneous series of images and ideas to flow in any order and in any direction. Make no attempts to censor yourself but simply fantasize and write whatever comes to mind.

- Notice any resistance to these suggestions and ask yourself what you find objectionable. Override each objection by reminding yourself this is simply a flight of fancy and that you are free to entertain any thought at all. Humor opens us to the unexpected, it exempts us from thinking logically and activates our imagination. Choose a serious topic and write humorously about its mood, its smell, its fate. Use any words that come to mind with no grammatical rules. Make no attempt to be logical or make a point. Do this as a game, something fun, not as a task.

- Imagine that some very important belief you hold has been found to be false. Then picture your life without the truth that was so important to you before, noticing how it would alter you, your choices, your relationships, and your ideals.

- See yourself in roles that you would not ordinarily play, both personal and political. For instance, you are a general in war or a successful nonviolent resister. Play the opposite of what you are.

- Imagine your childhood totally free of all restraints, from either family, school, religion, or peer pressure. Picture yourself acting in ways that match your new liberty.

- Imagine that your parents are your children.

- Imagine a house with wind for walls, ocean for floors, earth for ceilings, and yourself as a permanent tenant.

- Imagine yourself as an animal, first as the animal you most like and then as the one you most dislike or fear.

- Imagine a fruit becoming an animal it resembles and then speaking to you in the voice of one of your friends.
- Imagine your hand becoming a claw, your arms becoming wings, your feet becoming paws. Then imagine describing your new body to someone you strongly admire.
- Imagine yourself flying through space, arriving at faraway planets, and meeting the diverse people who live there.
- Imagine that you are visiting a cemetery and raising a friend or relative from the dead. Dialogue with him or her about the afterlife, but not the one that is familiar to you from religion.
- Imagine that you are the most dangerous criminal in your hometown and that you are ready to give yourself up, but only after one more crime.
- Imagine yourself to be of a different race, religion, gender, or sexual orientation. Picture yourself in your daily routine but as that altered person. How does this experience affect your stereotypes of others?
- Imagine an owl morphing into a zebra, then a baseball bat, then an oil well, then a bike that you ride out onto the sea without sinking. Switch these five morphs to other objects as you prefer.
- Imagine that all you ever wanted is now yours but that no one else exists on the planet.
- Look out your window at the familiar scene and repeople or reorganize it in any way your fancy may take you. In "Song of Myself" Walt Whitman is alone and "the scenery is plain in all directions." He then says, "I fling out my fancies" and imagines a battlefield, encampments, and finally a cityscape to fill in and alter the monotonous landscape. Imagination gives us the freedom to begin with what is actual and get to what is impossible.

You are taking parts of us into places never planned.
— ADRIENNE RICH, "FINAL NOTATIONS,"
FROM *An Atlas of the Difficult World: Poems 1998–1991*

5

Facing Life's Emotional Challenges

> I am grateful to God for giving me this gift, this possibility
> of developing myself and of writing, of expressing all that
> is in me. I can shake off everything if I write. My sorrows
> disappear; my courage is reborn.
>
> —ANNE FRANK

Most of us have not taken advantage of the comfort, help, and healing that come so naturally from writing a poem when we face challenges. In this chapter, we look at six of the most common issues in life and learn ways to write poems that might help us find comfort and face them. The six issues are fear, loneliness, depression, addiction, childhood memories, and relationship concerns.

We can begin by looking at how most of what concerns and distresses us has two sides. We usually have a conscious knowledge of our issue. There is, however, also a hidden or unconscious dimension. A poem begins with a conscious intention, but as we flow with our writing, we tap into our unconscious and find out more than we might have guessed about who we are and what is going on. This is why writing poetry can help us so much in self-discovery.

The same distinction between conscious and unconscious applies to our motivations. The reasons we do what we do and make the choices we make seem entirely thought-out, but there is an often secret agenda that is being followed too. This means that it could seem as if we wanted to clear up a problem, consciously, while unconsciously we really want to keep it just as it is. For instance, we may want to stop smoking, but unconsciously we fear what life would be like without the relaxation—or escape—provided by a cigarette. We may want to marry someone because we love her, but unconsciously we want to work something out with our mother. Consciously we seek a sequel, a new story, but unconsciously we seek a remake of the old one. We may consciously desire to break up with someone. Yet, unconsciously we want to stay long enough in the relationship to take revenge for all the hurts we have endured, or to keep hurting ourselves for how unworthy we think we are, or just because hurt is all we know.

Our Conscious Motivation:	Our Unconscious Motivation:
On the surface, known to us, what we think is driving us	Deep within, unknown to us, what is also driving us
Seeks satisfaction and fulfillment	Seeks resolution and completion
Wants to stay and enjoy	Wants to let go and move on
Demands comfort	Accepts challenges

As we rally our writing powers to compose a poem, it is helpful to keep the above chart in mind, to presume there is an unconscious motivation afoot somewhere, and to realize that our poetry may give us a clue to it. Throughout this book we have noticed that we are most successful in writing a poem when we combine mindfulness, openness, and imagination. Usually our mindfulness shows us what is happening consciously and our openness and imagination steer us into the deeper waters of the unconscious. This is yet another reason that the combination of mindfulness and imagination that happens in poetry can make for a degree of healing and resolution that does not happen ordinarily.

Now we can look at specific difficult stresses and explore how writing poetry can lead to more confidence in handling them as well as healing any wounds they may have caused us.

Fear

Fear is the distressful feeling that happens when we are in danger or believe we will be. Most of our fears are in our heads rather than

in reality, but knowing that makes no impact on how painful it is
to feel them. The chart above applies to fear in that our motivation
may be conscious and unconscious at the same time. For example, we may consciously fear commitment to someone but unconsciously fear closeness to anyone.

It is a rare day when a fear of some kind, real or imagined, does
not stop by. We can use the "Triple A" technique:

Admit we are afraid
Allow the fearful feelings to happen fully
Act as if—or so that—fear cannot drive or stop us

For instance, say we have been out of work for months and fear
that we will not land the job we have just applied for, the first—and
only—one that has come along.

Here is an example of writing a poem that simply admits what we
fear. Using the techniques we have learned so far in this book, we can
write a simple rhythmic admission that we are indeed afraid. We combine mindfulness, or attention to the here and now, with imagination.
We sit at our desk and see a peony outside our window. We look at it
mindfully, with no particular thoughts or judgments. Then we open
our imagination and write in poetic form. Here it is as a sentence in
prose: "I am afraid I won't get the job." Here it is as a poem that combines our predicament and the reality we see in nature:

I must confess to you, peony,
I'm scared of being poor
So hide me in your thousand petals.

Now we have admitted we are afraid, but also, *just in the writing,* perhaps we noticed that the generous number of petals on the
peony has added the healing realization of personal abundance.

Even looking at a cactus can help, by the way:

I must confess to you,
Cactus in the dust,

I'm just as scared
As you are alone.

A poem does not have to give comfort in any obvious way, nor
does it have to cheer us up with hope or the vision of a silver lining.
Since our psychological work begins with admitting where we are,
just stating our condition has something beneficial in it.

Our fear of being jobless for much longer than we have been may
lead to a string of consequences in our minds: we will not be able
to pay the rent; we will be embarrassed about our failure; we will
have to borrow money from friends; we will become homeless; and
so forth. Our logical mind knows that these things are not likely
to happen, but our fear keeps raising the possibilities of all kinds of
danger and disaster. We can allow ourselves to see the humor in our
catastrophic thinking. Then we may write a humorous poem about
it. Chuckling at ourselves releases pent-up energy and diminishes
stress. For example, the monologues of late-night talk shows often
take serious topics from the nightly news and discover the humor
in them. We ourselves can imagine exaggerated consequences of
our fears by stringing them out in our minds to the point of absur-
dity and thus smiling at ourselves.

Finally, we can notice where a fear is in our body and write our
poem from that location. In prose we may say, "I know I am scared,
because my stomach is churning." Here is a poetic style of stating
the same idea:

My fears are butterflies
Who can't get out,
At least not yet.

When I wrote this, I stopped after line two. Then I felt I was not
telling the whole story and line three came to me. I was not manu-
facturing hope by adding that line. I was recalling the human given
that things can change, the Buddhist truth that all is impermanent.
I may not have thought of the comforting "not yet anyway" if I
had not been attempting to write a poem. This is an example of

how the unconscious fuller truth can arise from our commitment to use poetry as a tool for growth. We access a nonlinear part of our minds when we write a poem, the region of imagination that presents hopeful alternatives and healing opportunities.

Loneliness

When we are isolated and lacking in human company or encouragement, we are actually not being true to ourselves. As mammals, we thrive on companionship and relationship. This is why loneliness is so hard to bear. There is no "For thou art with me," an essential ingredient for survival.

In depression, our feelings are unexpressed, as we shall see below. In loneliness, our feelings are up and running. Thus our lonely state can be a good beginning for journaling about how we feel. Loneliness is not a feeling. A more accurate description is that it is a state of mind. Rather than saying: "I feel lonely," we can more accurately say, "When I am lonely, I feel ...." We might complete that sentence stem with words such as *abandoned, rejected, deserted,* or *discarded.* However, these are not feelings either. They subtly judge those who have abandoned or rejected us. They describe states of mind and mood rather than actual feelings. Our simple Anglo-Saxon words express our feelings: *mad, scared, glad.* These also happen to be the words that make our poems more accessible and impactful. Those two characteristics are forms of reaching into ourselves and out to the world, and those are, in themselves, healing options when we are lonely.

We might think or write, "Here I am alone, abandoned by my friends and family. They have discarded me as useless or unwanted. I feel angry at them." This anger is actually an appropriate part of grief, another way of describing the essence of loneliness. We are sad, angry, and afraid that we will not recover companionship. These are the feeling components of grief. Here is a way to begin a poem: "Now I am lonely and I feel sad, angry, and afraid."

We can notice as we write whether we are blaming anyone for our loneliness. We move toward statements that keep the responsibility for how we feel on ourselves rather than on others. Carl Jung wrote that loneliness is offset by a sense of our own completeness. When we are lonely, we lose that sense. We feel we are only half alive, because an important part of us, the part that requires relationship, is unfulfilled. As we take responsibility for our own loneliness, we find the completeness that can assuage it. We cannot make others want to be with us, but we can want to be with ourselves.

We also notice that as we bring our attention to our experience in this way, we may automatically feel a companionship with all the people in the world who are feeling as we are. We notice that it is in the archetypal nature of humanity to feel forsaken sometimes. We are now gaining a sense of connection with all humans at all times and in all places who have felt as we do now. This is itself a release from our loneliness, because it is a yes to a given of life that unites us all. One of the spiritual practices of Buddhism is called loving-kindness or *metta* practice. In this practice we send loving-kindness first to ourselves, then to those we care about, then to those we feel neutral about, and so forth, ever widening our circle of compassion until it includes all beings. In this practice, as we saw above, we make contact with all other humans who suffer as we do, and we ask that we and they find happiness, equanimity, love, and compassion.

We can examine our use of words like *abandoned, rejected, deserted,* or *discarded.* We can notice how they point the finger at those who seem to have forsaken us. We can transform our words into embraces by our declarations and aspirations of loving-kindness. Our poem can take the shape of a move toward loving-kindness and actually be a way to *perform* the practice. In traditional loving-kindness practice, we make the following statements, starting with ourselves and widening out to others:

> May I be free from danger.
> May I be happy.
> May I be healthy.
> May I be at ease.

We can use this form as a point of departure to make a poem about our loneliness that moves us toward loving-kindness, growth, and wisdom. Here are some examples:

May my sense of abandonment be mine with no judgment of others.

May I not abandon myself but stay with myself by feeling my authentic feelings of sadness, anger, and fear.

May I hold these feelings as mine with no accusations of others.

May I benefit from this lonely time as an empowering phase of my own journey.

May I join with all beings everywhere who feel as I do. May they too be empowered.

May I and all those who are lonely feel our real feelings and move through them to a sense of completeness in ourselves just as we are.

May I find companionship in my own energy and in my own sense of wholeness.

May all my friends and family find wholeness too.

May all beings be free of loneliness.

May all beings have an enlivening sense of their own completeness.

May I and all beings be joyful, loving, compassionate, and even in temper in the face of all that life brings.

Depression

When we are depressed, we feel hopeless and helpless to change our mood. Our creative skills may not be much in evidence. Our sense of despair may overtake our ability to access pleasure. We lose our faith that "this too will pass."

Depression can be the result of an ongoing physiological problem. It can also be associated with a recent loss. Grief comprises three feelings: We are sad that something—or someone—important to us is gone. We are angry that it was taken away. We fear that it may never be replaced. When we are depressed, we lose our ability to activate, express, and thereby resolve these feelings. They are in us but can't move through us and be released, as feelings are meant to do.

In addition, depression affects our appetite, our sleep patterns, and our energy levels. We are at the mercy of a downturn in our entire life and this lack of control adds to our sense of helplessness. We may also feel worthless, since our sense of worth is associated with our competence and ability to function well. Thus, our self-esteem takes a beating in any depression. Sometimes, therapy and drugs can be of help, but depression has a life and timetable of its own in any case.

In the midst of depression, we may not have much interest in writing a poem at all. Perhaps we can, however, simply scribble down the truth of our condition. For instance, we can write, "I'm too depressed to write a poem." Just putting this statement on paper is helpful, because it makes a firm declaration, and that firmness is a sign that there is strength in us. Such strength is itself a first step toward change.

We can take our simple sentence and write it this way:

> I'm too depressed
> To write a poem.

We can look at these two lines and see them as a poem. So we add, "Yet here it is." Now we have a poem indeed:

> I'm too depressed
> To write a poem
> Yet here it is.

In coming up with a poem—of any kind—we are retrieving our competence. This may make a contribution to our self-esteem. Such an experience is the opposite of that helplessness that is so depressing.

A poem will not necessarily release us from our doldrums, but it is a beginning. It is beginners' mind at work, a Buddhist way of describing how we can approach our condition without control, expectation, judgment, shame, or demand for change. This style is mindfulness, an attention to the bare reality of our predicament without our usual inhibiting framework of concepts and wishes.

We may experiment with writing about our very mind-sets in depression, or our response to our depression. This, too, can become a poem. For instance, we can list these three statements;

> I want control over my depression.
> I am judging myself as worthless.
> I have to get out of this.

In mindfulness, we let go of those embroideries around our pure experience, the mind-sets of ego. A pure experience is a complete experience, one with nothing around it but space. *We then manage our reactions while learning from them, not putting ourselves or others down for them, and not having to act on them.* We may rewrite our statements this way:

> I let go of my expectation that I will be able to control my depression. I accept that I am not in control.
> I let go of judging myself for my depression. I accept it.
> I let go of my demand that I be released from my depression. I accept its timing over my own wishes.

These three acceptances locate us in our actual condition of depression. They can become a poem that serves as an affirmation, a practice that can be of help in finding healing:

> I let go of trying to control this,
> I let go of judging myself,
> I let go of demanding an end or explanation.
> I accept my own reality,
> I am free of shame,
> I honor timing.

Depression often vanishes as mysteriously as it arrived. A daily simple reshaping of whatever statement we can make about how we feel may lead to a sense of recovery of creativity, and that can fly us to some hope, "a thing with feathers that perches in the soul," as Emily Dickinson noticed.

Addiction

Addiction happens when we become dependent on a person or thing in such a way that we are compelled to keep seeking it. We tragically seek satisfaction without ever finding it fully. Indeed, addiction is a search for the *transcendent,* something that might fulfill us in an impermanent world. Since it has this spiritual dimension, it requires a spiritual program as a path to recovery. A higher power than ego takes the place of alcohol, for instance. We're never fully "cured" of an addiction, but we can be in recovery for the rest of our lives as long as we refrain from acting on our compulsion and rely on powers beyond our ego.

In Buddhism and in many spiritual traditions, attachment is seen as dangerous to our happiness and well-being. Addiction is just such an attachment. It can happen with regard to alcohol, drugs, sex, gambling, relationship, or any number of objects in life that seem to offer an escape from or softening of the blows of reality.

We are usually attempting to get away from the givens of life, the unavoidable facts of living, namely, the challenges of changes, endings, unfairness, and pain. Our addictions are attempts to escape these givens as well as our feelings in the face of them. An addiction offers a respite that seems to be a remedy. The problem is that the remedy is temporary, like all things else in this limited and fragile world.

An addict usually believes that he can handle his addiction, or that she can control her use of a substance, for instance. This is the ego's way of asserting its power. But it does not take long for any addicted person to notice that his life has become unmanageable. Then, hopefully, he can admit his powerlessness and rely on a power greater than himself to restore him to sanity.

Twelve Step programs, such as Alcoholics Anonymous, are remarkably successful, since they offer a path toward release from the ego and its addictions. The Steps include taking a moral inventory of how our addictions may have hurt others and then making amends. They also recommend developing a relationship to a Higher Power as an alternative way of handling the givens of life.

The final Step of the program moves the recovering person into compassion and service.

The Steps are elegant spiritual practices that help us make three transitions. The first is from a life of dependency and addiction to a life of sobriety and freedom. The second is from a rugged self-reliance to a willingness to rely on something transcendent. This transition is not from dependency to independence but rather to healthier forms of interdependence, for example, learning to turn to a "sponsor" or to others who are also recovering. It moves us from ego to the Higher Self, or to God, or whatever we understand that transcendent power to be. The third transition is from selfishness to service, as described in the Twelfth Step: "Having had a spiritual awakening as the result of these Steps, we tried to carry this message to alcoholics and to practice these principles in all our affairs."

The program and the Steps lend themselves to the writing of poems. The moral inventory and list of amends, for instance, are meant to be written. We can keep a journal of our progress in the program, using poetry as a way of telling the story of our journey toward recovery.

A narrative poem is one that tells a story. We can write our autobiography in the form of a poem. We can make it as long as we want at first. Then we can rewrite it, giving only one stanza to each decade of our life. Finally, we may rewrite it again, giving only one line to each decade. We may also, or instead, want to write a memoir of a meaningful event connected to our addiction.

We can also write a poem to express how we feel about finding the program itself. In this way, we bring our creativity to our experience. This is a way of enriching our manner of resolving our issues. We resolve and expand at the same time.

When we express poetically what is happening in our therapy or our recovery program, we find more depth in ourselves. This is because as we write, we draw from what was unconscious before. Then facts and insights arise into consciousness, and our sense of what is happening to us and of what has happened to us becomes more intense, more vivid, and hence more empowering. This combination of personal conscious work by writing poems and dredging up information from our unconscious is what is meant by "finding meaning." Our experience is more meaningful to the extent that it pulls together the present moment of awareness with the past moments that arise into awareness. Then the here and now embraces all our days and all our story. This is how awakening finally happens. Poetry is a nudge in that direction.

Childhood Trauma

In chapter 3, we explored the theme of childhood and its influence on our adult choices. We used a visualization that may have helped us heal some of our past. Now we look at how memories of our childhood, some of which evoke pain or regret, can be worked with in a more specific way and how writing poems can be beneficial as part of that process.

We all notice memories of our childhood arising from time to time. They may be calls to us to pay attention to something from the past that is ready to be looked at and resolved. They may be aroused by similar events that are happening in adult relationships now. Much of what happened to us in early life left us with a sense of incompletion. It takes mindful attentiveness and the working through of the feelings associated with an event for that experience to be resolved, completed, and let go of. Otherwise, we may be doomed to unconsciously repeat in adult relationships what has been left incomplete from our past.

Earlier I presented a four-step program for healing and change—addressing, processing, resolving, and integrating—and discussed how that process can manifest in writing a poem. Now we can apply that program to childhood memories.

To *address* is to look carefully at what happened and call it by name. To *process* is to go through the feelings that the experience evoked as fully as we can. In addition, we notice whether we have transferred onto a person in our life today some of the emotions or expectations related to the past. To *resolve* is to let go of any blame of others or shame about ourselves for what occurred as we make a plan for change. To *integrate* is to implement our new consciousness into our daily life so that it can no longer interfere with wholesome living and relating now.

Here is an example: Let's say your father sometimes beat you when he was drunk and your mother did not intervene. You can *address* that painful memory now by calling it abuse related to alcoholism. To address leads to acknowledgement of the fact, realization about the characters in the story, and understanding of the overall issue: You can acknowledge how deserted you felt when your mother did not protect you. You realize that she did not come through for you because she was probably too scared to do so. You can see this as a feature of an alcoholic family. This does not excuse it, only helps you understand.

To *process* this memory is to allow yourself to feel the feelings that may not have been safe to express in your household. These feelings may be sadness, anger, and fear, the components of grief about any loss or abuse. Finally, you ask if you yourself have an alcohol problem or are in a relationship now with an alcoholic or addict of any kind. Are you re-creating the past by playing any of the three roles: persecutor, victim, bystander?

To *resolve* what happened is to refuse to repeat the past, to let go of blaming your parents while acknowledging their accountability, and not to retaliate now. This is a gesture that makes you strong enough to imagine yourself speaking up or defending yourself in those past scenarios. Finally, you are resolving not to let the same thing happen to you again, nor to do it to others, nor to let it happen to anyone you love. If you need help, you are choosing to go to therapy or to join a recovery program.

You *integrate* the past memory when you can look back at it with an unconditional yes to the way it was rather than a fantasy of how it was better or worse. You can see it with compassion and even some humor. You can live as one who has lived through pain and become better for it, the essence of heroism. If you are in recovery because you have repeated the past, you are staying with it.

At each stage of this psychological practice, you can be writing your experience and letting poems emerge. You can write a poem during or after each of the phases of addressing, processing, resolving, and integrating. This evinces more information and feeling from the unconscious, and you may be surprised at how your long-repressed memories begin to come back to you. When they do, they can be journaled as poems too.

Poetry brings healing to the past when we find ways to revisit it through what comes out automatically as we write. For instance, in the example above, you may recall a time when your dad slapped your face so hard that your neck hurt for the rest of the day. You write this:

> That Saturday—
> The vodka—
> Your hand so swift, so hard,
> My neck still hurts.

Your memory was of how the slap hurt *for the rest of the day,* but your pen wrote "still hurts." That phrase alerts you to the lasting quality of the abuse. This becomes a metaphor for how the events in childhood did not end when they happened but have continued into the present. In a way, your neck is still reverberating. For instance, your phrase may now give you an insight into how your dad's abuse has lasted into the present. You recall that you are on guard when someone becomes angry with you now. You turn away or try to smooth things over. You are protecting yourself from an unconsciously expected blow, even though it is unlikely to happen now. This leads you into more important information about your relationships and your fears. The poem helped get you there, or rather, here—that is, got you to who you are now but no longer have to be.

Some of our memories may be too painful to recall fully. We may not be ready to address, process, resolve, and integrate what happened to us. It is important to honor your own timing and not to probe too deeply when it seems that you are not yet ready to handle what may be revealed. This is where psychotherapy can help by providing a container in which your memories can be safely explored, held, honored, and at last examined.

As we recall our unfulfilled needs in childhood, we may notice how they resemble our present needs in relationship. We may experience loneliness and neediness for a relationship. We write in our journal of how we feel, using simple fourth-grade words and lines in a poetic format. This accesses our right brain, where imagination opens into a spaciousness that replaces the void. This is part of the addressing program that actually helps our feelings change and moves us toward more self-sufficiency. Gradually, we become less needy and are able to locate our true adult needs rather than those that are holdovers from childhood. Our poems become a way of charting our progress toward liberation from neediness by recording how we feel in each new twist and turn. Then we notice that freedom from neediness is much more exciting than immediate fulfillments. Progress in poetic journaling helps us move in that liberating direction.

Relationship Concerns

A good way to begin writing poems to our partners may be through composing valentines. However, we do not have to wait until February 14 to send them. Any note that shows our love can mean a lot to our partner and can bring more intimacy into the relationship.

As we saw in chapter 1, our original needs in life were the five A's: attention, acceptance, appreciation, affection, and allowing. These were provided by our parents fully, partially, or not at all. Poems can certainly flow from our recollection of how the five A's were or were not given to us.

These very same needs are the ones we bring to our adult relationships. We seek a partner who will give us what we needed from the beginning of life and still need now: someone who is committed to paying attention to our needs and feelings, accepting us just as we are, valuing us as individuals with all our limits and gifts, showing affection in physical ways, and allowing us to grow in accord with our own deepest needs, values, and wishes. When this happens in a reciprocal way, it is love, authentic intimacy, and true commitment. When one or more of the five A's is missing, we will feel the loss, because we instinctively desire these gifts, and we always did. Love poems help us express the five A's to our partners, and may evoke poems written to us in return. In general, it is a useful practice in a relationship to write each other poems that tell what is happening within us. Just as the president gives a "state of the union" message on a regular basis, we can do the same. We write our message about the state of our personal union in the form of a poem. We share this with our partner, who does the same. It may feel embarrassing at first, but it will soon become easy and even enjoyable.

We can write such a poem in five stanzas, each one referring to one of the five A's, how it is being expressed to us, and how we believe ourselves to be expressing it to our partner. It summarizes the state of the union from the point of view of intimacy. Here is an example of a poem that touches on each of the five A's:

> You noticed when I was feeling depressed last week, [attention]
> Not demanding I snap out of it, [acceptance]
> Accepting that I won't always be right here for you
>   [acceptance]
> And valuing me anyway. [appreciation]
> Your hand on my shoulder yesterday meant a lot [affection]
> As did your allowing me not to have to talk. [allowing]

That poem tacked onto the fridge when you leave for work can mean so much to your partner, who may have been wondering what was going on with you. The poem reveals you and your state of mind and heart.

It is sometimes a good idea to leave poems on a fridge, bureau, mirror, or table so that the other can read them on her own when you are not there. A partner can then experience her own reactions and contemplate the poem in her own way. Your presence is in the poem, and when your physical body is present too, it can be a distraction from the delicate you that is revealed in the poem. A partner's realizations and declarations about you and the relationship may not happen as easily when you are standing there waiting for a response. A partner can then write a poem in response or simply choose to talk about it when she sees you next. Her own poem may come later.

Poems can also be written on anniversaries to sum up the high points of the year. They can be written to commemorate important events and milestones in the relationship. On birthdays they say so much more than a standard card may say. Poems are primarily forms of communication. Writing poetry to one another in a relationship thus increases the scope of our dialogue.

Each poem we write has a unique intention and will be read by someone with a unique interpretation—just the kind of communication that happens in a relationship. Poetry is an enrichment of intimacy that we have not perhaps appreciated fully. The suggestions in this book may help build our relationships at the same time that they may be building our own sense of who we are. A poem, like a heart, tells more than words can say.

6

Poetry and Spirituality

It is a steadying thing to realize that one's personal work links with entirely natural phenomena, the universals, and what we expect to find in the best of poetry, philosophy, and religion.

—D. W. WINNICOTT

I am a magnificent hymn,
The meter of a sacred chant.

—*Bhagavad Gita* 10:35

In this chapter we explore further how poetry can help us to grow not just psychologically and emotionally but spiritually as well. What do I mean by "spirituality"? A truly conscious spirituality makes us more fully alive in the here-and-now world, with a concern for all its personal, political, social, and ecological implications. Indeed, Carl Rogers considered psychologically healthy people to be the "fit vanguard" of human evolution.

Spirituality, a word related to "breath," "life," and "energy," does not mean becoming otherworldly. A spiritual consciousness refers to any action and awareness that fosters the qualities of integrity, compassion, and love in unconditional ways and to a universal extent. This includes:

• Being liberated from our ego's illusion of separateness, entitlement, and self-centeredness
• Making our life a heroic journey from egocentricity to self-giving

- Accepting the givens, seasons, and transitions in life with a hearty and unconditional yes
- Contacting and cherishing the basic goodness in ourselves, in others, and in all that is
- Finding the bridge between experience and its transcendent significance
- Acknowledging the emptiness from which all arises and into which it sets as a vast and harmonious spaciousness in which we all participate
- Trusting the mysterious and enduring presence of divine or spiritual powers that always and everywhere assist us
- Showing appreciation and thanks for the work of grace in our lives

As we've seen, many items in this list are automatic and integral to the writing of poetry. Indeed, poetry writing can be understood as a form of spiritual practice: When we write poetry, we make the journey from our version of "how life should be" to a fidelity to "how it is," trusting that it is unfolding in just such a way as to lead us to our destiny. In writing poetry we come to understand that any single experience or reality is simultaneously a manifestation of ourselves, of nature, and of the divine life. In this chapter we'll explore some of the many connections between poetry and spirituality.

Synchronicity

Synchronicities are meaningful coincidences. What makes it possible for us to perceive synchronicities is our ability to recognize meanings in dreams and events, to see analogies between what happens in the world and what happens within ourselves, to read the signs in unusual correlations, to be open to significances and purposes that seem external but resound interiorly too, to notice pointers on our path, to notice how things are lining up so that we can notice and appreciate the inherent goodness in all that is. This is how our inner life blooms and then makes its debut in the world.

Poetry is like synchronicity in that it arises from a combination of chance and meaning. By chance someone dies and a poet writes a poem about the loss, finding a meaning she never guessed was there. We read the poem by chance and find a meaning that fits for us today.

Our challenge when we experience synchronicity is not to figure things out but to open to what will be revealed on its own. That skill is exactly what it required for writing or appreciating poetry. Thus the artistry in appreciating synchronicity is the same as that in poetry.

Synchronicity shows that events that seem unconnected—like a poem from the past and a here-and-now meaning to a reader—come together in a pattern that is significant. Poetry is synchronicity in words, since a meaning emerges from patterns that combine thought and feeling, as well as conscious and unconscious themes. Both poetry and meaning expand and contract, like the breathing that is the focus of meditation. All these combinations are examples of synchronicity as well as of the art of poetry. Indeed, Gregory Bateson described our aesthetic sense as "responsiveness to patterns that connect."

That sense is the same in spirituality. We respond to what connects us to one another. This connectedness is based on the wise realization that we are one as a human family. We share the same genetic code and the same code words and images that define who we are. We notice images in our dreams and in our imagination that are archetypes—common themes—in the collective life of humanity. This similarity is a meaningful coincidence, a synchronicity that points us to our spiritual bond. Gandhi used the term "heart unity" to refer to our ineradicable and innate oneness. This unity comes to life when the wisdom of no separation is joined to loving-kindness in our choices. Synchronicities gather when we make that commitment. We begin to meet up with just the people and events that challenge and stretch us to love more.

Synchronicities show that more is afoot in our human enterprise than can be explained by human choice or control. A unanimous spiritual realization is that something, we know not what, is always at work, we know not how, to make us more than we are now and to make the world more than it is yet. We then feel held in a grace-filled universe, as if we were the children of it, not its victims or rulers. With that humility, we are ready to be launched into our full capacity for wisdom, love, and healing—accurate descriptors of the "something we know not what." Synchronicities happen to move us in that sacred direction. They are the signposts on the spiritual path.

An elegy, a poem about a person who has died, arises from a poet's personal experience and memory. The theme of her poem certainly hearkens to us from the collective unconscious, since it locates patterns known to our ancestors, expressed in similar images and in similar artistic symbols of grief. She also speaks as a seer and prophetess, one who sees what *we* will feel if a similar event happens to us. The connections and patterns wait to be enacted in the chords and rhythms of poetry. The reader relates and connects as the synchronicity continues.

The poetry we write draws from the silo of images of all humanity. We become one with all the poets of the past in our mutual quest toward understanding ourselves and our purpose. Perhaps they are even helping us, like heroes and saints whose lives encourage us. Percy Bysshe Shelley understood the archetypal nature of writing poetry: "Every poem is an episode to that great poem, which all poets, like the cooperating thoughts of one great mind, have built up since the beginning of the world."

Every poem elicits meaning out of chance, a flight of meaning out of pedestrian occurrences, a host of daffodils out of a garden of imagination. We are exuberantly welcomed there and then are delighted to say yes. Every poem is an exciting example of synchronicity, because every poem connects past, present, and future. Every poem happens at the right time and place. All we have to do is be present, that is, to allow a meaning to come through to us or from us. Some of our work is effortful. Some is simply allowing. In the visualization that follows we will see how we can align ourselves to that possibility.

VISUALIZATION

Allowing What Wants to Happen

Use the preparation in chapter 3 and follow up this visualization with journaling, writing in easy lines so that a poem can result. Revise the lines more and more so that the elements of poetry appear: rhythm, sensuous images, figures of speech, economical language, and unrestrained imagination.

You are noticing that you can jump off your own train of thoughts. To get off that train and stand here on the platform of silence can be very calming.

You can stand here not particularly waiting for any other train. You can even stand here not waiting for someone to get off the train.

You can just be on the platform. And if a train goes by, you can notice that the train goes by.

And if no train comes, you're not feeling impatient, because you're not waiting for a train. And if no one gets off the train to meet you, that will be fine with you, because you're not expecting anyone.

And if a train should stop here, and someone you know should get off, and hug you, that will be acceptable too. You'll be happy to receive that greeting.

And if that person then leaves and goes his or her own way, you'll be able to handle that too. And if you decide to walk away together, you'll be able to do that with no sense of fear of what might come next.

You are trusting that everything happens at just the right time and place.

You're standing on this platform noticing you have no fears of what might arrive next in your life.

If a train is coming to meet you to take you away, that will be OK. If a train passes you by, that will be OK. If no train comes, that will be OK. You are simply letting yourself be with what is. You're saying yes to what is, as it is.

You've let go of trying to control or even know the schedule. You've let go of trying to make the trains in your life run on time.

You've let go of trying to make people walk over to you. You've let go of trying to keep people away from you. You can accommodate their getting close; and you can accommodate their going away.

And when someone goes away, you notice that your fear of abandonment is not that overwhelming.

And when someone gets close, you notice that your fear of engulfment is not so strong.

You're allowing other people to go away. You're allowing other people to stay. You're letting it all be OK. You trust that comings and goings all happen at the right time and place. You are trusting the power of synchronicity, meaningful coincidence.

You're letting whatever others may do become something you can take in stride, accommodate flexibly, something you can surrender to, with no attempt whatsoever to get others to change their minds, to keep them away from you, to prevent them from going so far away.

Instead you're simply noticing what they do. You are the fair and unblaming witness of them and of yourself. And you're witnessing with the attitude of yes. Here on this platform of nowhere special.

It feels good not to be waiting, not ever having to wait again, not to have to wait for someone to come across the tracks for you, not to have to wait for someone to get here just at the time when you wanted him or her to be here.

You are happy not to have to wait for someone to get on the train and go away. You are simply letting yourself be with all comings and goings. You are trusting they happen in meaningful ways and line up perfectly with your own journey.

And you are letting this very platform support you in your surrender to what is or will be.

You notice you don't fall through. It's safe to stand. It's safe to be with what comes and goes, without having to make anything come or go.

You're feeling safe here with all the changes and coincidences. You can stand, you can dance, you can move.

You are still and still moving. You are free to move whether or not there are people in your life. You find yourself on the platform with such a clear realization: You have never really missed any train that matters.

As the following affirmations arrive in your mind, you're feeling stronger, more able to nurture yourself, more unafraid of what may happen:

I am content to stand. I am content to go. I am content to stay.
I am content to let someone go. I am content to let someone stay.
I am content to be already and always here.

Now you are returning to this time and place, bringing your consciousness back from this platform in your mind, returning to the here and now, thoroughly refreshed. When you're ready, take out your journal and write. Use the elements of poetry so your lines can shape themselves into a poem.

Poetry and Nature

Look deep into nature and you will understand everything human.

—ALBERT EINSTEIN

When we interact with nature, we may sometimes sense human meanings. This congruence of the natural and the personal is a common feature of spirituality. We feel at one with the world, nothing interfering, nothing intervening. Such a realization leads to the joy of knowing our identity as not separate from everything else. In fact, there is no "else."

Poems employ metaphors, whereby two things become one in meaning. This is how the nondual, or the not-separate, shows itself in creativity. We can see how nature connects to our human story through metaphor in this short poem of mine:

These poppies
Bow:
Priests in red vestments.

Here we notice oneness immediately, because the redness of the poppies can be the same as the color of religious vestments. The metaphor compares the poppies to priests. Both bow, one to the

wind, one to God. The comparison implies that nature and God are
one and that the flowers are sacred. They are here to perform sacred
rites for us, as priests do. Priests are considered mediators between
people and God, though they are mortal. Poppies mediate eternal
beauty to us though they are ephemeral. Poets mediate wisdom
though they are ordinary folk. Since the priests are vested in metaphor, they are also poets, so the poem can be about poetry too. We
also notice that all this comes through in seven words, showing how
economy works with metaphor to enrich a theme in a poem and
render it provocative.

The poem evokes spiritual themes as we are alerted to our connection to nature and our priestly role in it. The bow has the sense
of humility and of honoring the natural world. We are thereby acknowledging and venerating the larger life of ourselves. We are
finding a resource for letting go of ego. We are locating a source
of self-soothing. These are elements of psychological and spiritual
growth.

Dag Hammarskjöld, the second secretary-general of the United
Nations, wrote of nature, "Here man is no longer the center of the
world, only a witness, but a witness who is also a partner in the silent life of nature, bound by secret affinities to the trees." Poetry can
express this affinity, our relationship to natural things. Poetry does
this with words, and also with rhythm and rhyme. When the author
Isak Dinesen lived in Africa, she sometimes spoke in Swahili rhymes
to the young natives. They broke into laughter each time they heard
a rhyme. When she stopped, they begged for more, saying, "Keep
speaking to us like rain." For the natives, rhymes came through in a
different way than ordinary speech did. They heard them as an el-
emental pattern from nature.

Nature is a common subject of poetry, since we humans are on a
journey *with,* not *in,* the universe. A poem is an attempt to attune
to the music of the spheres, the harmonies in the universe that transcend individuality and yet reconnect it to the whole.

According to the Zen tradition, when the Buddha attained enlightenment, he proclaimed, "I and the great earth with all its beings
simultaneously have become enlightened." Poems about nature cut

through appearances to reach into the what-is of things, to their awakened state, to their basic goodness. To enter such poems thus becomes a crossing of a threshold into the light that is enlightenment.

Zen Master Dogen said,

> When your [spiritual] practice is authentic, the sounds and shapes of the valley streams and mountains all turn into verses of the scriptures . . . . Ask the trees and rocks to preach the Dharma [the Way] to you. Seek the truth in rice fields and gardens.

Here is his poem:

> Entering the heart of the Sutra,
> Are not the sounds
> Of the bustling marketplace
> Also a proclamation of the Dharma?*

Nature is the cosmos, which comprises space, time, matter, and energy. Its impact can be welcome, the way daffodils are, or perilous, like earthquakes. Nature and poetry are bedfellows, because both enter those alternating realms and bring us there to *stay* and *see* whatever may be, the two purposes of mindfulness. In mindfulness practice, we stay by continually returning to our breath. We see by noticing the ultimate emptiness of our ego-driven thoughts.

This realization of emptiness is the threshold into enlightenment, a space that opens when fear and grasping cease. Soon, in any place in nature we discover the same threshold into spaciousness. The eighteenth-century New England preacher Jonathan Edwards mused, "Surely there is something in the unruffled calm of nature that overawes our little anxieties and doubts. The sight of the deep-blue sky,

---

* From Steven Heine, *The Zen Poetry of Dogen: Verses from the Mountain of Eternal Peace* (Boston: Tuttle Publications, 1997).

and the clustering stars above, seem to impart a quiet to the mind." That is the mind of mindfulness.

Animism, the belief that all things have a soul, signals humans' long-standing need to be related to the natural world. Thus, connecting, a spiritual goal, is an innate drive, part of our autopoiesis, our self-becoming. Primitive practices demonstrate this: trance, shamanic drumming, summoning spirit helpers, speaking secret and animal language (imitating animal cries and bird songs). These are all examples of rhythm, the framework of poems. Poetry likewise begins with a secret language, a personal diction that is a code. It shuffles and tumbles ordinary language but ultimately reveals the essence of things.

Science can tell us so much about nature and how it works. Yet, we find out something about nature in a poem that cannot be found in any scientific lecture. Science is "study-about"; poetry is "entrance-into." Notice this exact point in a superbly crafted poem by Walt Whitman, "When I heard the learn'd astronomer" (*Leaves of Grass,* 1900):

> When I heard the learn'd astronomer;
> When the proofs, the figures, were ranged in columns before
>   me;
> When I was shown the charts and the diagrams, to add, divide,
>   and measure them;
> When I, sitting, heard the astronomer, where he lectured with
>   much applause in the lecture-room,
> How soon, unaccountable, I became tired and sick;
> Till rising and gliding out, I wander'd off by myself,
> In the mystical moist night-air, and from time to time,
> Look'd up in perfect silence at the stars.

This poem, like all meaningful poems, speaks to a part of us that cannot be reached by science—our soul. The poem is lyrical, imagistic, metaphorical, experiential, evocative, personal, mysterious rather than simply explanatory. It appeals to us physically and sensuously. It has a shape on the page that is pleasing and inviting, unlike the paragraphs in a scholarly article or lecture.

The poem uses words differently from the way they are used in an essay. In an essay, words are chosen to make a point clearly. Here the writer unabashedly wants to please our sense of aesthetics and expand our appreciation of his personal experience.

We notice that the tedious lecture is to be heard, whereas the stars can be looked at and we thereby know so much more about what they are—and who we are under them and among them.

The poem uses the word *unaccountable* to contrast direct experience with "the charts and the diagrams." We see the play on words, since an "account" has to do with numbers. The fact that the mind cannot account for the move the poet makes from the lecture hall can be a reference to grace, a power that helps us to evolve. It is also a visitation by the muse who led the poet to writing this poem. We notice, too, that the lecture is heard in a group but the mystery of the stars is found by wandering off alone.

Finally, the word *gliding* shows that the poet is not in control but rather is being carried by the creative spirit from the hall of science to the art in nature. This is quite intriguing a reference, since the word *glide* is actually used in the original Hebrew in the first sentence of the Bible to describe the act of creation: "The Spirit of God *glided* over the waters."

A person walks through forests of physical things that are also spiritual things, that watch him affectionately.

—CHARLES BAUDELAIRE

VISUALIZATION

Seasons and Transitions

Use the preparatory suggestions in chapter 3 for this visualization. After doing this visualization, immediately write about your experience in your journal. Notice how what you write can become a poem.

You are in the woods in the peaceful late afternoon.

All the animals are at rest after their hunting. They are browsing or relaxing, free of fear or desire.

You can see older animals and younger ones. Some of the animals move slowly; some are lively. You can tell what phase of life they're in by how they move.

You like it here because you can be here safely. The animals don't see you, but you can see them. You see the mothers with their young; you see some of the young nursing. You see how the mothers take care of them. You see the fathers standing guard, or drowsily lying nearby.

You observe animals in their adolescence. You become aware of their playfulness. You're noticing how different and yet how much the same they all are.

You can see that this is a chain of life, and that it's acceptable here to be old. It's acceptable to be young. Age doesn't matter, because it's all happening simultaneously and cooperatively. You are admiring that.

You have a sense that this is a life-and-death place. Death can happen here at any time. You're noticing that that's all right. You can see there's no attachment here, yet so much caring. You admire that.

You're noticing the silence. There are no words here, and yet the scene as a whole says so very much.

There are no thoughts here, just an instinctive surrender, an unconditional yes to every moment, whatever that moment brings.

No one knows how to say "I love you" here, but they nonetheless act in a loving way.

There's no battle with reality here, just an acceptance of it. This you admire.

If it rains, they will know what to do. If the sun blazes intensely, they will know what to do. When night comes, they will not be afraid, because they're at home everywhere here, at any time here, in every season here. You notice this.

You're noticing that they are abundantly alive. There are no blocks, no ambitions, no repression, no guilt, no poses, no disguises, no addictions, no partial existence, no partiality.

Every energy here is committed to life, to an affirmation of life, to true presence. There is no refuge here in the past, which is no more; nor in the future, which is not yet; there is only now. In fact these animals' very survival depends precisely on their being here now, totally awake, totally pleased with themselves and the world.

No sense of neediness here. No attachment. No plan. No regret. Just presence. You're admiring this.

You're glad to be here among them. They call you to another way of being. And if you were to hear this call, you, too, would be blessed with some of these wonderful things: presence, fearlessness, contentedness, harmony. You can see they want you to have this. They want you to live in the present.

They offer you the power to do this. You say yes to this, invoking their power.

You feel the instinctive side of yourself. You appreciate your animal nature, your animal body, your place in the animal world. To this you say yes.

You are happy to know that nature belongs to you too, not just to them. They share it with you. To this you say yes.

You're rejoicing to be in their presence and to share in this power. To this you say yes.

You are going to the place in you that is not caught up in attachment, the place that is unconditionally present, that knows how to take care of yourself, that feels at home in nature. To this you say yes.

You're here in the wilderness in your inner mind and you hear yourself affirming:

I commit myself to life as it is.

I am in touch with my instinctive, earthy nature.

I love the seasons of my life.

I enjoy my age.

I bring more silence to my life.

I thank these animals that have come to me.

I take them, or one of them, as my guide to empower and assist me in my future.

I ask their forgiveness in the name of all mankind, for how we have hurt them.

I picture my arms around a tree now and I hear myself saying, "I am the same as you, changing and unchanging, passing and everlasting."

I came here through the spaces between my breaths, and now I come back to my present world through these same spaces. This time, instead of falling through my breaths, I rise up between them with power to care, to be present, to be here now, to pass beyond appearances, to find eternity in the present and infinity in the place where I am now, nothing less than heaven on earth. To this I say yes.

Now you are returning to this time and place, bringing your consciousness back from this guided, faraway world, from this forest in your mind, returning to the here and now, quite refreshed. When you're ready, begin writing in your journal. This will be a poem.

Poetry and the Transcendent

The pleasure of reading and writing poetry helps me God-ward.

—THOMAS MERTON

Poetry is the sound an event makes when it lands in meaning. When we read or write a poem, we are touching into meanings that relate both to us and to our world. To find such meanings is part of the spiritual path. This is because poetry can be a bridge between experience and its transcendent significance. This bridging realm, "the between," is precisely where spirituality flourishes. It is not tied to any single polarity, but is alive in the connection between them.

Our personal unconscious contains the experiences of our own life from birth until now. The collective unconscious is the repository of the ancestral experience of all humanity, our heritage at birth. In this collective treasury are stored primordial images and themes that appear to us in imagination, dreams, and creative arts such as poetry. The images are artistic, visionary, and spiritual—like those we see in religious iconography. The distance between human and divine is highly overdrawn, and art, like prayer, hangs in that seeming gap.

The transcendent is reality beyond appearance, form, or ego. It cannot be grasped or appreciated by linear or logical rules, since it abrogates and exceeds them. Likewise, poetry can use transitory experiences to locate or express transcendent themes. We, too, look at transitory things in nature and understand our transcendent destiny through them.

The concept of poetry as sometimes mediating divine wisdom was recognized by Plato in the dialogue *Ion:* "All good poets . . . compose their beautiful poems not by art but because they are inspired and possessed. . . . God uses the minds of poets as his ministers, as he also uses diviners and holy prophets, in order that we who hear them may know them to be speaking not of themselves, uttering these priceless words in a state of unconsciousness, but that God himself is the speaker and that through them he is conversing with us."

When we write from poetic imagination, we access the transcendent and we incarnate it into our here-and-now world. This is why poetry is a threshold, on which we stand with one foot in the here and now and the other in eternity. *All it takes to feel it is a letting go of our limited mind and a letting loose of our unlimited imagination.* Since poetry cannot be written or read in any other context than freedom from limitation, it is perfectly suited to the transcendent.

We can sometimes feel how a poem's rhythms are calibrated to the tune of eternity and to the rests of space, at once those of the universe and our own. Lorenzo, looking at the stars, says, in the speech from Shakespeare's *The Merchant of Venice,* "Such harmony is in immortal souls." Perhaps this same harmony is what we found in infancy in the safe arms of mother, and now sometimes seek in the world of nature. The harmonies of repeated rhythms in a poem effect that same oceanic embrace. Indeed, creative impulses aim at just that.

Joseph Campbell asks and answers a question: "How does the ordinary person come to the transcendent? Study poetry." He was perhaps echoing Ralph Waldo Emerson, who expressed it this way: "Poetry was all written before time was, and whenever we are so finely organized that we can penetrate into that region where the air is music, we hear those primal warblings, and write them down."

A theme in this book is that poetry reflects who we are and shows us how to find out about ourselves. We know, for instance, that the psyche operates at a variety of levels: personal, collective, transpersonal. Poems can be interpreted at those same levels. The poem below by the sixteenth-century poet Sir Philip Sidney is about two people in love and thus is personal. Yet it takes us to the collective experience of humanity that shows how individual love has a spiritual dimension. Indeed, mystics in medieval times spoke of an "exchange" of their hearts for the heart of God, the very word used in the poem. Perhaps this was a way of affirming that love is the medium by which the human and divine are one?

On another level, the poem is about the transformative experience of the spiritual journey we all make. We give up our ego heart in favor of the heart of the higher Self. We give up our selfishness in favor of loving-kindness. Sir Philip Sidney may not have planned his poem to express all this, but the very fact of writing a poem opened him to other dimensions. This is the transcendent power of poetry.

In his conscious mind, the poet intended this poem as a valentine. But a higher consciousness than the poet might have noticed took shape in the words so that they revealed layers of meaning that reflect the wide spectrum of human possibilities. A poem has a mind of its own. This is how a poem synchronously talks back to a poet and opens his work to a wider world. A meaningful coincidence occurs between his experience and the release of hidden meanings from and about it. All our experience is a metaphor for vaster prospects than we might dare to glimpse.

> My true love hath my heart and I have his.
> By just exchange one for the other given:
> I hold his dear, and mine he cannot miss;
> There never was a bargain better driven.
> My true love hath my heart and I have his.
> His heart in me keeps him and me in one;
> My heart in him his thoughts and senses guides:
> He loves my heart, for once it was his own;
> I cherish his because in me it bides.
> My true love hath my heart and I have his.

Freedom from Division

Art can transcend apparent oppositions. The operating principle of the unconscious is described by Carl Jung as "enantiodromia," the innate ability to contemplate apparent opposites, hold them both, and dance with them (another reminder of the value of poetic rhythms). The fact that we do this means that our practice of poetry is simply an alignment of our ego choices with what wants to happen in the farthest reaches of our psyche. In this way, we experience opposites as complementary rather than contradictory. Then we know that all that is in us is arranged in just that way.

For instance, it seems that male and female, life and death, the psychological and the spiritual, the earthly and the celestial, are all polarities. But in reality they are intertwined, all part of one cycle and thus united like partners in a tango, intense yet graceful. The analytic mind sees them as opposites, which helps us understand their differences psychologically. The archetypal Self sees them as one, which helps us situate their meaning spiritually. This is another way of seeing the necessity of spiritual consciousness if we are ever to appreciate the full meaning of being human. The materialist view is reductionist. Full science, that is, full-spectrum knowledge, of ourselves and the world, takes more than the standard scientific method to reveal itself, just as a poem takes more than analysis of words to be understood fully.

Nonetheless, the style of logic is to divide reality into parts. It configures pairs of opposites not as correlatives but rather as polarized and warring tensions. These ego-fed oppositions find an opportunity for resolution at night in dreams and during the day in our poems. (The spiritual urge was always to dissolve oppositions but not distinctions, so our logical mind did not really have to worry in any case!)

The practices and exercises in this book facilitate our contact with the transcendent. The spiritual is not located in some other-worldly realm far away from us. It is beyond location, hovering here in our poetic words and in the themes they portray, hovering "overhead" only in the sense that it is beyond what ego can control or coerce. Our work is simply to unleash our spirituality by freeing ourselves from our dualistic thinking and from our false belief that anything at all is beyond the ken of our imagining. Then apparent oppositions coalesce and unity appears. This is how spiritual consciousness readies us for poetry and returns us to it.

Opposites combine in the very composing of poetry, since our writing is at once:

Controlled: entirely as we imagine it and saying what we wanted to say	Uncontrollable: taking off in its own direction and conjuring up larger meanings than we imagined
Consciously thought of and written	Summoned up from the unconscious
Understandable	Mysterious
Carefully crafted	Spontaneous
Using words accurately	Defying grammar to find new meanings
Mindful	Imaginative

Here is a story that leads us to one final point: Three men were working in the fields in the heat of noon when the bell rang from a distant chapel. The first man said, "Oh, good, it's time for lunch!" The second man said, "What a beautiful sound; I will write a poem about it!" The third man simply stood in silent awe. Our goal in this book is to write from our silent awe.

Beautiful moments and things in nature say, "Stay with me." This is one way that spiritual realities address us. At special moments in life, we may sense that something transcendent is coming into the present through us. Such a spiritual visitation happens as a grace, an inspiration. We are asked in those moments to help the psychic presence become embodied, to bring it into consciousness and let it communicate with us, and maybe with others too. The poem we will then write may accomplish that spiritual task of incarnation.

A muse is an archetype of inspiration, grace to release our creativity. The muse will knock at the door but is not likely to stay for a visit with a lazy host. This certainly resembles our task in becoming healthier, both psychologically and spiritually. It takes work and practice, but we can trust that grace *wants* to come through, both for us and through us.

One becomes nothing but a medium for super-mighty influences. That which happens can only be termed revelation; that is to say, that suddenly, with unutterable certainty and delicacy, something becomes visible and audible and shakes and rends one to the depth of one's being ... as in a storm of feeling, of freedom, of power, of divinity.
—FRIEDRICH NIETZSCHE

EXERCISES

Three Practices

We often write poems based on a subject, for instance, something that has happened. Try writing a poem cold, with no preparation and with no topic in mind. Simply write freely and see what comes through. Poems often arise from unconscious motivations. The poem you write today may bring up answers to questions you may pose only later, since in the unconscious there is no time. Writing a poem when you seem to have no specific reason to do so may reveal what is incubating within you, something ready to arise from the unconscious and become known.

———

The Psalms are poems that are prayers, and many poets have written poems that are prayers. If this fits for you, base a poem on a phrase from a prayer or spiritual reading and/or write a poem that is a prayer. Example 2 in the appendix shows you one way of doing this.

———

Plato taught that our innate inclination to transcend ourselves, in order to grasp what the world is about, is called "eros." It is a primordial connectedness that leads us to seek contact and to enter the mystery around and outside us. This becomes a transcendent experience as we pass beyond ego. Many mystic poets have shown the close connection between the erotic and the spiritual. Write an erotic poem and then apply it to God or whatever stands for the divine in your spiritual worldview. Here is an example from the Bible (New International Version), *The Song of Solomon* (4:5–7):

> Your two breasts are like two fawns, like twin fawns of a gazelle that browse among the lilies.
> Until the day breaks and the shadows flee, I will go to the mountain of myrrh and to the hill of incense.
> All beautiful you are, my darling; there is no flaw in you.

In more modern poetry, look at this example from Walt Whitman, from his poem "I am he that aches with amorous love," from *Leaves of Grass,* 1900):

> I am he that aches with amorous love;
> Does the earth gravitate? Does not all matter, aching, attract all matter?

Stillness and Movement

Throughout this book we've seen how both mindfulness and imagination must be cultivated in order to write a meaningful, healing poem. Mindfulness is stillness. Imagination is movement. The combination of stillness and movement is a spiritually effective style for how we live our lives too. We refuse to be caught up in activity but are committed to frequent pausing, taking time to let things unfold. Writing a poem thus reflects a spiritual balance.

We notice how motion and stability combine in the Greek statue entitled *The Discus Thrower,* which was originally sculpted in bronze by Myron in 460 B.C.E. In this work of art, we see the athletic body poised like a taut bow; yet the whole sense of the figure is one of utter serenity and equanimity. The athlete is excitedly competing, but he also remains totally pacific, focused, and self-composed. His pose is poise. He is passionately engaged in a graceful and directed movement. At the same time, his body is arched in deeply meditative repose. This is the combination of opposites that characterizes the best art, be it sculpture or poetry.

Discus thrower (Roman copy of a bronze original.)

Such a combination of opposites also characterizes us when we find psychological health and enter the spiritual realm, the twin goals of our evolution toward wholeness. We combine our psychological work, which takes effort, with our spiritual openness, which takes allowing. The ego–Higher Self axis that happens in such individuation is visible in the combination of action and acceptance.

The statue is motionless, but the movement bursts through, not only in how the sculptor's imagination brings it to life but in the mysterious sense of motion he has achieved. This may be what the poet Rilke meant by "outer standstill and inner movement."

There are moments in which we are neither all motion nor all stillness. Instead, like the discus thrower, *we experience a perfect stillness in our motion and a perfect motion in our stillness. This is the combination of mindfulness and imagination that represents the essential practice in this book.* Such a combination of seeming oppositions is how poems warm up and then hurl themselves to their victorious goal.

Poetry is not only a product; it is also a happening, like life and its purpose: I am not here just to *do* something but also to let something *happen* through me. What I do leads to the joy of accomplishment. What I allow leads to the ecstasy of opening. As I combine effortful movement and patient stillness, I make contact with the wholeness—both psychological and spiritual—already and always within me and everywhere around me. This is the fruit of mindfulness, and it takes imagination to see it as a possibility for any of us. The building blocks of our poems are found in that quarry.

7

Reading Poetry for
Growth and Healing

When you love something, you understand it.

— GERTRUDE STEIN

We have to be initiated into reading poetry, and this is sometimes painful since it means letting go of our ego's need to make sense of everything and to understand all that is happening. When we give that up, we are on spiritual soil, because we have opened to what wants to happen, to the messages of a surprising world, to moments of enlightenment.

To understand a poem, it is not necessary to know what is meant by every word but rather to flow with the themes, rhythms, images, and significances that keep bursting through. We can appreciate the *Mona Lisa,* while still realizing that we will never understand all its symbolism. Likewise, to understand ourselves, it is not necessary to know what everything in our lives really means but rather to flow with the rhythms and significances that keep bursting through.

Though a poem can lead to uncertainty, we can sense a coherence. A good poem presents us with a truth here and now. In fact, a poem, like a spiritual practice, is a "now" experience. A poem only fully exists while it is being read by someone. In this sense, too, poetry and the reading of it are related to what happens in mindfulness, a steadfast allegiance to the here and now.

Poetry we read initiates a verbal, visual, and tonal journey, but not into clear fact. Rather we find ourselves drawn into meditative suspense. As we read and ponder with concentration, attentive hearing and seeing, we are ferried into a participation in the poet's own feeling and the depths of meaning he or she is uncovering.

Since a poem presents us with symbols and metaphors that are endlessly provocative, we cannot simply expect a one-size-fits-all meaning or one that fits once and for all. Indeed, to interpret a poem means to recognize the presence of something ultimately unknowable and to be satisfied with that—a true test for the ego, which, as was said above, wants to be in control by understanding every word fully. A letting go of that need and a profound bow before a mystery are rich openings into the spiritual world. The philosopher Martin Heidegger said, "The poet lets words be"—as does the wise reader. *Could there be a better description of human serenity than that same "Let it be" to all that we may see?*

We miss so much of a poem when we are mainly concerned with nailing down exactly what it says, like looking at a beautiful bird only to know its species. Interpretation of a poem may bring us closer to its cognitive meaning, but that simultaneously may distance us from its mystery. Yet a full meaning includes both. For example, notice the double meaning in words deriving from the name Hermes, the Greek god who bridges the heavenly Olympic realm and our earthly plane: The word *hermeneutics* refers to interpretations geared to understanding. By contrast, the word *hermetic* refers to something secret that cannot be understood fully. The words of a poem combine, and sometimes confuse, what is known with what cannot be known. They reflect the anatomy of our psyches: known and unknown, clear and complex, past and present, conscious and unconscious, comprehensible and incomprehensible, all at once.

We can learn how the strands of comprehension in reading the words of poetry come together in Ezra Pound's *The ABC of Reading.* He distinguishes three forms of poetic meaning:

Melopoeia is the melodic sound and rhythm of a poem. This refers to *how* something is being said. Since poetry is music in words, mellifluous words and pleasing turns of phrase make the lines dance. We read a poem to join a dance already in progress. Not all poems today place a value on beautiful words, but rhythm is a part of all poetry.

Logopoeia is the cognitive meaning that ultimately lets the poem make sense to us, even though we may not grasp the full intent of every word. This is about *what* is being said. Modern poems, especially confessional or autobiographical ones, are sometimes too subjective or personal to be understood fully, but the main theme certainly comes through to us.

Phanopoeia results from the picture-making power of the poet. This refers to the *images* that are being evoked. Sometimes, they are personal to the poet and/or to us. Yet this feature of poetry can cross time and national boundaries, because these images are common to all humanity.

Why Are Some Poems So Hard to Understand?

A limit happened perhaps in school, when we noticed we did not understand the poem being discussed the way the "smart kids" did. We may have given up on poetry or on ourselves: the grapes are "sour anyway," so why bother trying to reach them. We "don't have what it takes to understand." But with work and help, anyone can understand. This chapter may provide the help if you are willing to work.

We miss the many-splendored work of a poet when we try to "analyze" a poem. In high school, we may have been taught to dissect and memorize. This got us off on the wrong foot. We did not thereby learn to appreciate poetry, only to feel in control if we understood, or obtuse if we could not understand—neither option helpful to our self-esteem or personal growth. In reality, when we focused on analyzing, we were using a flat screwdriver on a Phillips screw. We were using our left-brain thinking spade to dig in instead of our right-brain intuitive springboard to dive in. Poetry takes us to the depth of feeling, a depth that dissection only trivializes. Poetry takes us to revelations about ourselves and the world that analysis or memorization only obscures. This is how poetry synthesizes, just like music.

We can appreciate the poetry we read as a chance to let go of having to know exactly what every phrase means, focusing instead on feelings and impressions, which are new and exciting priorities for most of us. We can appreciate the poetry we write as a chance to disobey the regulations of our discursive mind, an exhilarating freedom from old limitations. In both instances, we may then take pleasure in involving ourselves in the mystery of a poem rather than in solving a puzzle. This involvement expands our sense of our own as yet unknown life and of its transcendent glories.

Many people feel intimidated or frustrated when trying to read poetry. This is usually because they are trying to read a poem as if it were prose, trying to understand each word and get a firm grasp of the total meaning. However, reading poetry requires a different approach. We enter a poem humbly, often without confidence about what it will mean. Yet when we stay with it, we notice a clue or two. Our confidence then increases and we begin to feel our way into the poet's intent and meaning. Poems are composed of clues and codes, but they want to be found and deciphered, so they reveal themselves to those who have patience and take the time.

A poem can make a serious point or satirize a serious point. Indeed, a poem can move in any direction at all. Since a poem is meant to be oral and aural, we do well to read it aloud at least once so that we can both speak and hear it. This can offer directions to us about the mood and premise of the poem.

Inasmuch as a poem emerges from a part of the brain that is not tied to discursive thought, it is not primarily detail-oriented but thematic and impressionistic. We respond to a poem with pleasure, and that's just as good as understanding it. We do not try to make sense of every word. There is usually a rational theme in a poem, but the lasting sense of it is what counts—and that is not always so easily explained.

The French poet Paul Valéry wrote, "The power of poetry is derived from an indefinable harmony between what it says and what it is. *Indefinable* is essential to the definition." Thus, something in a poem will always elude our grasp. Appreciating a poem means surrendering to a mystery. Reading prose demands a thorough comprehension. Reading poetry frees us from that obligation.

Poetry comes through the way music does, not the way words do. Beguiling rhythms seduce us, and unnamed feelings sweep us away from our ordinary mind-sets. We let music speak for itself. We hear the sounds, we hear the notes, and we focus on them with an attentiveness that is as pleasurable as the music itself. When we do this in reading poetry, we are satisfied with symbolic or metaphorical meanings rather than explicit ones. We miss the many charms of a coquette when we insist that she yield her mystery to us all at once. Poetry is just such a lady.

Freud said that poetry is a kind of dreaming. Indeed, poems are usually written in a compressed way, coming at us like witty dreams, at times not fully lucid in meaning, often employing a puzzling and mirthful juxtaposition of images and characters. We are met with startling surprises, mismatches, cunning metaphors, multiple and sometimes contradictory levels of meaning. Wouldn't this be an exciting way to live more of our life?

There is a paradox within poetry and within dreams: A limited number of words and images can alert us to unlimited possibilities. A dream, like a poem, both reveals and conceals. A dream told or written is always a poem, since it is freewheeling, not necessarily logical or syntactically correct, full of intriguing symbols and metaphors, exciting without having to be fully understood.

Good poems, like dreams, leave gaps to be filled in by our own subjective improvisation, rather than telling us everything. The more we appreciate poetry, the more we enjoy this feature. Our concern is not with an obvious explanation but with how every word adds to the impact of the poem. Images in poems are often holograms, not discrete components of a linear series. Our lives do not have obvious explanations, and each experience is a hologram indeed, complete in every moment, a record of light. Surrender to this marvel is what discovering depth is about, how it flourishes, how we are true to it.

Wallace Stevens wrote, "A poem is a pheasant disappearing in the brush." An incomprehensible poem is simply frustrating. But the elusive feature of a poem is part of the fun of it. The words of a poem skirt the meaning, since the meaning defies, tricks, and jokes with the language. A poem may also be hard to pin down because the emotion it presents may seem unacceptable, unfitting, or unnameable. The language used in poetry can then make it acceptable. An example is the phrase used by Sylvia Plath to describe suicide:

"the big strip tease." The dark ironic humor somehow lets the unappealing thought become *bearable and suitable*—puns intended.

In any case, we do not fully know anything simply by an intellectual grasp. Knowledge, and certainly wisdom, take intuition too. Concepts analyze and separate realities like words in a vocabulary list. We need a way to see how all is connected, and that requires our poetic sense, a combination of intuition, feeling, vision, and imagination. That combination is reminiscent of spiritual wisdom, not tied to analyzing and dividing, the favorite pastimes of the ego. Indeed, our analytic intellect can only say, "I get it." Our syncretistic poetic sense says, "I see how it fits." Our personal sense says, "I see how it fits for me."

It is legitimate to ask, "What does this poem mean?" We further enrich our experience of a poem when we also ask, "What does this poem mean to me?" The poem by Walt Whitman about the astronomy lecture is easily understandable. It is a greater challenge to ask what personal impact it has on us, how it changes us, how it invites us into a novel way of seeing or living. Then it speaks to us about our life now and here, rather than only about the experience of a poet at a lecture long ago. Again we see how poems connect past and present.

A poem can leave us wondering what the poet really meant. That is so much like life, like relationship. We wonder what events, words, and feelings meant, and sometimes we never know for sure. Yet we can remind ourselves that some experiences are too profound and incomprehensible to be understood fully. We can only stand at the threshold, the in-between space where human meetings happen. It is the same place in which poetic fires ignite.

Indeed, poetry may be vague, not because it is confused or because we are not intelligent enough to understand it. Poetry may be unclear because the skill set of the thinking mind and its dictionary definitions have failed. In poetry we're moving beyond mind, another indicator that we are venturing into spiritual territory.

Zen Buddhism speaks of the importance of cultivating a "don't-know mind," which refers to letting go of our compulsion to know what everything means, dropping our preconceptions, and being

willing to experience life freshly and directly. Reading poetry requires this kind of don't-know mind. As we become healthier psychologically, we don't compulsively seek the safety and security of
concepts and mental knowledge. We begin to trust in our feelings
and in something larger than the intellect. Poems that do not per-
mit full understanding challenge us to grow in just such trust: "I
don't get this poem fully, but I feel this poem; I sense a mood in it; I
enjoy it. This is satisfactory and ample."

When T. S. Eliot says, "Poetry communicates before it is understood," he reminds us of the experience of mystics. Like poets, they
too leave explanations behind, because the need for them has vanished in the flash of experience. Perhaps feeling a poem rather than
fully analyzing it can reveal a path to mystical awareness. Indeed,
giving up having to know or control everything in a sure, certain,
conceptual way means that only pure awareness with no particular
focus remains, a high form of mindfulness. This is how mystics of all
traditions were able to glimpse in the dark night of any chaos and
confusion an irrepressible dawn of divine life permeating all that is.
In fact, "all" becomes singular, no longer plural.

Here is a poem ("Stanzas on Ecstasy in High Contemplation")
by the Spanish mystic Saint John of the Cross that affirms these
realizations while inviting us to feel with what is said rather than
analyze it (this is my own translation):

> I entered I knew not where,
> And there I stood not knowing:
> Nothing left to know.
> I had entered the house of unknowing
> And knew not where I was.
> What great things I heard
> I cannot tell;
> I was there as one who did not know:
> Nothing left to know.
>
> Of peace and devotion
> My knowledge was perfect,

My solitude profound.
So secret was it
Even I could only stammer.
I had nothing left to know.

I stood beside myself in ecstasy enraptured;
My senses vanished, every one.
I had the gift of understanding,
Yet was I understanding nothing:
Nothing left to know.

The higher my achievement,
The less was left of me.
All that I had known
Was worth but nothing now.
This new-born wisdom grew
Till I knew nothing in any final way
And had nothing left to know.
The higher I ascended,
The less I comprehended.
O dark fog that gives the night a glow.
To understand is not to know
When there is nothing left to know.

This knowing that knows nothing
Has such power
That reason can't defeat it,
Or ever penetrate the depth of heart
That understands the nothing left to know.
What sovereign wisdom this is,
Beyond what science can ever attain!
He who dares to go beyond the mind
To the Knowing—Unknowing,
Always will come back alive,
But with nothing left to know.

Only listen and this wisdom
Reveals itself: a voice from heaven!
Ah, it was divine compassion all along
That left me naught to know.

Prose and Poetry, Mind and Heart

I wish our clever young poets would remember my homely
definitions of prose and poetry: Prose is words in their best
order. Poetry is the best words in their best order.

—SAMUEL TAYLOR COLERIDGE

The words in a poem love showing off. They draw attention to
themselves like showgirls. In poetry, words lift their skirts. In ordinary prose, words are not presented to be hovered over or gazed at,
since the accent is on getting a point across or relating a narrative.

A poem electrifies words so that they impact us more forcefully
than ordinary prose can. The words in a poem do not adhere to
their definitions. A poem wants us to cherish its words, to live with
them, to dance to them. They contain volts and BTUs. The diction
of poems is minted from images, rhythms, unusual choices of words,
vagaries of grammar, and figures of speech such as metaphor and
simile. For instance, we can speak of getting old in this way: "I am
not what I used to be." Now look at this same thought in these two
lines from Shakespeare's Sonnet 73. Notice how much more of an
impact they make and how they are so much more memorable than
the original sentence:

That time of year thou mayst in me behold . . .
Bare ruin'd choirs, where late the sweet birds sang.

Ordinary prose can be one-note, saying what it means and only
that. The multi-meanings in words become a resource to the poet.
Robert Frost said, "Poetry provides the only permissible way of saying one thing and meaning another." Unusual ways of using words,

presenting richly arresting images, offering intriguing multi-meanings, all with dense economy—these are ways of describing poetry. With this definition, our life story is in poetry rather than in prose. Our life was never meant to be one-note, but instead rich with variegated meanings and unusual experiences. Our life, like poetry, no longer has to be bound by the limits of narrow goals or constricted definitions. We can believe in our own immensity. We automatically keep transcending limits as we evolve into our fullest selves. Poetry does that too and takes us along as we read it with respect and diligence. In fact, poetry does in words what evolution does in us:

- We begin with mindful attention in order to contact our own here and now
- Then we open our imaginations to the images, metaphors, and meanings that poems present
- In the richness of imagination and in plumbing the unconscious, we find personal meanings in the treasury of images that we have inherited from our ancestors, universal symbols that reveal the fingerprints of the soul

Look through your journal of poems to locate and appreciate the unfolding themes and how they reflect the three points above.

Coleridge comments that poetry can evoke "a more continuous and equal attention than the language of prose aims at." Can this be a comment not only on poetry but on how we can live our lives more freely and fully? We keep noticing that what the best of poetry can do is also the best we do. Every fact about poetry is a fact about ourselves and how we grow.

Poetry requires so much effort from us because it tends to be implicit rather than explicit. For instance, a prose essay explicitly analyzes a fact, while a poem synthesizes a fact with a feeling. As we become psychologically healthier, we no longer allow facts to lie fallow by resting in any single dimension. We work with facts so that they become more than simple data. We find rich meanings in them and integrate the feelings they arouse. We thereby become people of more depth. We have more going on in us than daily, routine thoughts and choices. We "see into the life of things," as William Wordsworth says. We see things in the luminous glow that issues from openness to the manifold layers of reality. We look for connotations, not only explanations.

A poem is certainly not comprehended only by the denotation of its words. It has to be entered through the looking-glass of connotation, that is, by our resonance with what the poet feels and what his or her words suggest. In that sense the connection between poet and reader is an empathic attunement. This can happen in prose too, but prose does not usually offer the depth of the implicit that poetry does.

Here is an example of how an empathic response in us can arise from an appreciation of the implicit in a line of poetry. We hear, "To be, or not to be: that is the question." As a philosophical statement, this simply means that the question we all face is whether to live or die. Yet in the mouth of Hamlet, with all the father and mother issues with which he is faced, it is so much more than a simple choice of life or death. The statement evokes questions about what sons owe to fathers and what sons may say to mothers. These feel like life-and-death issues to a prince who is a student though his father has asked him to be a killer. The "to be" of Hamlet is a commitment to follow through on revenge. The "not to be" is a disappointment to the memory of a father so dear to him. In a poetic context, a simple prose statement becomes quite far-reaching.

Thus, there are many implications in Hamlet's "To be or not to be." We discover an implicit treasury of meaning that words take on when spoken by a conflicted human about his destiny. That is what makes "To be or not to be" a line of elegant poetry rather than a mere ordinary sentence.

Hamlet's lover, Ophelia, appears onstage at the end of the speech. What force of terror, surprise, and compassion would the words have in her ears? She certainly shows compassion for her lover's woebegone state. We too, in the audience, feel sympathy for the young prince. We care about his choices and his jangled fate, so out of tune. We see our own story in his. Poetry makes Hamlet and us kin, and kinship is the connectedness that spiritual practice seeks. Again we notice the alignment of appreciation of poetry and spiritual progress.

Anything personal to us has implications as meaningful as those of *Hamlet*. Our own poems and those of others allow us to explore those depths, as we will see in the poem below by Emily Dickinson. We begin with a summary of her poem's theme expressed in prose: "The day after someone we love has died, we clean up our home and sadly realize the finality of death."

Now notice how this same point is made in a poem:

> The Bustle in a House
> The Morning after Death
> Is solemnest of industries
> Enacted upon Earth—
>
> The Sweeping up the Heart
> And putting Love away
> We shall not want to use again
> Until Eternity.

The prose sentence says exactly what the poem says, but it only states a premise. It is simply informative. In the poem by Emily Dickinson, something altogether more powerful comes through: an immediate feeling in rich ornaments of images, metaphors, and rhythms that animate the action being described. In the poetic version of our original statement, we sense that we have been invited into an experience, whereas in the prose sentence we are simply being notified. The prose statement is an explicit disclosure of an observable fact that can be accepted in a detached way. Prose tells us. Poetry shows us. Poetry is a revelation of the hidden mystery in the fact. It stirs us to involvement. Prose makes us observers. Poetry makes us participants.

Notice that neither the prose statement nor the poem are stated in personal terms. Yet the poem is somehow personal while the prose declaration is not. How does this happen? The poem achieves a personal dimension by the *intimate dialogue* the poet opens with us in order to share her meaning-laden and feeling-rich experience.

The poem is also personal in that we know that the poet knows that the word *hearth* is expected but has placed *heart* in its place. The word *love* takes the place of *guest china*. Both words are affectionately warm and the words they replace are homey. We feel closer to the poet and can empathize more easily than if she spoke the original prose sentence, which is accurate but not so warm. The poet has achieved closeness between herself and us, no minor feat in only thirty-four words.

The prose sentence we read only once to grasp the entire point. Prose hands us a final report. The poem we will want to read many times and it yields new insights each time. William Wordsworth stated this in *Lyrical Ballads*: "Verse will be read a hundred times whereas prose is read once."

Prose is not the opposite of poetry. The opposite of poetry is discursive thought. Most prose is just that. But there are exceptions. Some prose is so well constructed that it can do what poetry does. We see this in passages from books or speeches that have been meaningful to us and to which we keep returning. In some novels, we find lyrical and meaningful passages that impress and commandeer us, as in those of William Faulkner or Herman Melville. Look at this soliloquy by Captain Ahab in *Moby Dick:*

> But it is a mild, mild wind, and a mild looking sky; and the air smells now, as if it blew from a far-away meadow; they have been making hay somewhere under the slopes of the Andes, Starbuck, and the mowers are sleeping among the new-mown hay. Sleeping? Aye, toil we how we may, we all sleep at last on the field. Sleep? Aye, and rust amid greenness; as last year's scythes flung down, and left in the half-cut swaths.

No one would doubt such powerful imagistic writing to be a prose poem.

> Clothed in facts,
> Truth feels oppressed;

In the garb of poetry
It moves easy and free.

—RABINDRANATH TAGORE

Three Poetic Styles

The style of poetry depends on the historical era. Here are three examples of poetry from one family, the Lowells of Boston. We can see how each poet uses language in strikingly different ways by considering the first sentence of a poem by each of them.

We begin with a poem by James Russell Lowell (d. 1891), "Prelude to the Vision of Sir Launfal":

Over his keys the musing organist,
Beginning doubtfully and far away,
First lets his fingers wander as they list,
And builds a bridge from Dreamland for his lay:
Then, as the touch of his loved instrument
Gives hope and fervor, nearer draws his theme
First guessed by faint auroral flushes sent
Along the wavering vista of his dream.

Here is the first sentence of the poem, "A Decade," by Amy Lowell (d. 1925), an imagist poet:

When you came, you were like red wine and honey,
And the taste of you burnt my mouth with its sweetness.

Now look at the first line of a poem by Robert Lowell (d. 1977) from "The Quaker Graveyard in Nantucket":

A brackish reach of shoal off Madaket—
The sea was still breaking violently and night
Had steamed into our North Atlantic Fleet,
When the drowned sailor clutched the drag-net.

The first example by James Russell Lowell places the emphasis on language that is meant to ingratiate and beguile the reader with its mellifluous sound. Yet the long sentence says very little and is mostly concerned with the beauty of the words rather than with presenting a challenging or absorbing theme. His poem is addressed to a general audience.

Amy Lowell's lines are direct and sensuous as well as economical. The point they make is clear. She chooses words that are beautiful but every one of them is important to her single focus. Her poem is addressed to a person.

Robert Lowell's lines are severe, with no attempt at direct lyricism or sonority. They do, however, express a mood that fits, but does not decorate, the theme. His poem is addressed to us.

We can see that each poet has extensive skill in craft but uses it in different ways. The craft of poetic diction is equally important to the success of all three poems, but it is too obvious in the first one. We notice the craft immediately rather than glide with it as a background to the theme.

At the same time, James Russell Lowell's mannered poem is more than just pretty words. It elicits the mysterious world of the unconscious and of collective realizations that arise when logic gives way to musical rhythms, which build "a bridge from Dreamland," the unconscious, from which a dawning light can be "guessed." Note that the poet himself may not have intended this perspective, but as we have been seeing, the poetic voice often evokes archetypal meanings that transcend conscious intentions of the poet or the poem. Jack's mother throws what she considers useless beans to the earth, but a heaven-touching beanstalk results. Poetry, like the events of life, encourages us to look deeply and trust that more will arise than we might ever have guessed.

In the second poem we see the craft but remain fully engaged with the story in the poem. The craft does not jump out at us but subtly supports the point of the poem. The words move with an erotic flow. The poet uses metaphor in a way that makes us focus on her point. She gives us, without embarrassment, a share in her physical delight in her lover. We even feel we can be the "you" who "came" into the relationship with her. We are encouraged to relate to the poem in intimate ways.

In the third poem, the craft of word choice is in the background, not intrusive as in the first example. The words begin in nature, and both the words and what is happening in nature set a tone for the story. We are drawn to enjoy the poem for its point and plot, not just its words. At the same time, we seem to be receiving an autobiographical revelation through the concerns the poet expresses in the poem. We are perhaps then encouraged to tell our own story and to appreciate how nature figures into the shape our life has taken.

We have thus found, in the first sentences of these three poems, three encouragements that relate to how we become healthier as people. They summarize our central tasks in becoming more fully who we really are. In the first, we were encouraged to *look deeply and trust that more will arise than we might ever have guessed*. To evolve personally and spiritually, it takes going below the surfaces of our life predicaments and experiences into the unconscious with all its storage of our story and that of all our ancestors. In the second, we were encouraged to *relate to the poem in intimate ways*. To evolve personally and spiritually takes connection with others in love and caring. This means opening ourselves to others and sharing ourselves both emotionally and physically. In the third, we were encouraged to *tell our story and to appreciate how nature figures into the shape our life has taken*. To evolve personally and spiritually takes a willingness to present ourselves as we are, in honest self-disclosure, while honoring the inner core that belongs only to us. Our personal evolution reflects—and grows from—that of nature with all its seasons and powers. Our life purpose is intimately connected to helping our planet endure.

The sequence in the examples above reflects the stages in the history of a human person as well as the stages in the history of poetry. We can certainly see a move toward more candidness in how poetry is written and in how we express ourselves.

All three poems were successful in the eras in which they were composed. Readers' tastes change and poets' styles change with them.

Or, perhaps, poets are like fashion designers, who lead the public into styles that induce them to develop new tastes.

Who we are as people is continually reflected in the way poems become less tied to forms and freer to be what they are, just what is happening to us in these times. The powers in society that clamp down on our freedom are often the same ones that fear or belittle the value of poetry.

Original and Familiar

> No matter what we may be doing at a given moment, we must not forget that it has a bearing on our everlasting self, which is poetry.
>
> —BASHO, *The Narrow Road to the Deep North*

Many poems express far-reaching, unexpected, and new realizations about the human journey. They relate commonplace experiences but expose the intensity of meaning and wisdom the poets have found in them. Yet a good poem does not have to be weighty in its conclusions. It can boil down to a simple, already well-known point. Here is Sonnet 55 by Shakespeare:

> Not marble, nor the gilded monuments
> Of princes, shall outlive this powerful rhyme;
> But you shall shine more bright in these contents
> Than unswept stone, besmear'd with sluttish time.
> When wasteful war shall statues overturn,
> And broils root out the work of masonry,
> Nor Mars his sword, nor war's quick fire shall burn
> The living record of your memory.
> 'Gainst death and all oblivious enmity
> Shall you pace forth; your praise shall still find room
> Even in the eyes of all posterity
> That wear this world out to the ending doom.
> So, till the judgment that yourself arise,
> You live in this, and dwell in lovers' eyes.

This is a masterly work, yet the main point it makes is not original but quite familiar. In fact, this sonnet reflects a work of the ancient Roman poet Horace. In the third book of his *Odes,* number 30, Horace uses almost the same words to make the same point: His beloved will live on after this mortal life by being memorialized in his poem. This did indeed happen, but the survival of literary memorials is not a new nor particularly profound realization in the annals of human wisdom. It contains a promise, perhaps meant to flatter someone, but it does not animate the human soul in any rousing way. Does this mean the sonnet lacks value? Not at all.

We can appreciate the poem, even though its message is so commonplace, since that fact makes room for the following other possibilities:

- The familiar theme reminds us that we all share a common sense of our relationships and a common wisdom about them and about life. The skill or intelligence of Horace or Shakespeare is not a prerequisite for wisdom. We have it too.
- The trite theme of the sonnet turns our attention to the *way* it has been composed rather than to a point we might overly focus on. Thus, we can appreciate the superb craftsmanship of the individual poet, noticing especially the deftness in the unique devices and diction. We thereby can appreciate the personal touch of the poet, another path to connection.
- We also see how a simple truth can be presented so elegantly and touchingly that it raises the shallow to the sublime, a pleasing combination of opposites.
- The fact that both we and the poet began with the same knowledge might encourage us to try our hand at expressing common themes in our own unique voice.

Because of all this and more, Shakespeare's sonnet is immensely involving and successful. And perhaps it may turn out to be quite personally touching after all, if we were to notice ourselves wishing that someone would write with similar passion to us! Poems can show us what we wish for.

Pleasure in the Words

Poems sometimes strike us as meaningful and memorable because of how well they are phrased. For instance, we might enjoy the following lines of William Blake, from his poem "To Mercy, Pity, Peace, and Love":

> For Mercy has a human heart,
> Pity, a human face;
> And Love, the human form divine,
> And Peace, the human dress.

Actually, more is happening to us than our being seduced by the rhythms and elegant simplicity of Blake's poetic diction. First, we are accessing a truth that has always resided in us. Secondly, we are being challenged to live in accord with the meaning in the words. The lines provide a description of who we really are, variously called our Higher Self, Buddha nature, Christ consciousness. The poet engaged us with words of beauty so that he could call us to our true nature. *We are learning how to be human.* Nothing less than that is the curriculum of poetry. The ingratiating phrases of a poem are the way a poet garners our attention. Then it is up to us to decide whether we want to live differently. In the example from Blake, this will mean to show mercy, pity, and love and so find peace. We see how poems can point to commitments.

At the same time, we always have the option simply of enjoying a poem without taking action of any kind. Poetry does not have to be about growth; it stands for what it is with no need for that or any known purpose. Poetry is not a harsh schoolmaster after all. It pleases those who want to be pleased. It calls those who are ready to be called.

Plato commented that a pleasing use of language can have a stabilizing effect on us and even lead to psychic integration. He saw the possibility of healing in the appealing words of poetry. Most of us who love poetry are pleased and even thrilled by language. Samuel Taylor Coleridge bravely stated that "the immediate object of poetry" *is* the pleasure of language. Read this last stanza from

"Frost at Midnight" in which he addresses his infant son, Hartley, sleeping in a cradle by his side:

> Therefore all seasons shall be sweet to thee,
> Whether the summer clothe the general earth
> With greenness, or the redbreast sit and sing
> Betwixt the tufts of snow on the bare branch
> Of mossy apple-tree, while the nigh thatch
> Smokes in the sun-thaw; whether the eave-drops fall
> Heard only in the trances of the blast,
> Or if the secret ministry of frost
> Shall hang them up in silent icicles,
> Quietly shining to the quiet Moon.

Now come back through the lines with me as we discover many subtle examples of alliteration (repetition of consonants) and assonance (repetition of vowels). You will see how the poetic diction is richly musical and can go unnoticed if we do not pay very careful attention:

> Therefore all seasons shall be sweet to thee, [four *s*'s, long *e*'s]
> Whether the summer clothe the general earth [four *er* sounds]
> With greenness, or the redbreast sit and sing [four *s*'s]
> Betwixt the tufts of snow on the bare branch [three *t*'s, three *b*'s]
> Of mossy apple-tree, while the nigh thatch [two *e* sounds, two *th*'s, and two long *i*'s]
> Smokes in the sun-thaw; whether the eave-drops fall [four *s*'s]
> Heard only in the trances of the blast,
> Or if the secret ministry of frost [three *s*'s, two *st* sounds]
> Shall hang them up in silent icicles, [continues the *s* sounds— even in the word *icicles*]
> Quietly shining to the quiet Moon. [continues the *s* sounds and adds three more long *i*'s to the *icicles* of the prior line]

We can appreciate how the intricate care given to word choice adds to the pleasure of reading and adds so much to the mood of the poem. Since Coleridge is a true craftsman, he did not force the word music on us but let it sound through—resonate—on its own. The patterns become clear as we read and reread attentively. They do not hit us over the head, but rather lull us with music.

However, this elegance in expression can be about much more than providing a reader with an opportunity to luxuriate in sweet words and mellifluous sounds. The alliteration and assonance of the words calm us and thereby show how poetry can have a healing quality. We can be soothed by poetry. Thus poems can offer tools, ways to become stronger in dealing with stress. We do not have to escape into our usual addictions; we can find positive ways to deal with tension. Poetry can be a resource when we're in need, a refuge from rigmarole.

Likewise, we can more easily engage with the theme of the poem and feel a kinship with the poet because the handsome words have commandeered us in that direction. This is another way that poetry is a force, both for personal healing and for connection with our fellow humans.

Since the poem joins exquisite words to a powerful theme, we are not simply lulled into oblivion but also confronted with challenging human issues: fathers and sons, the world and its future, the wish for happiness and the fact of frost. Just as life combines comfort and challenge, so does the poem. This is how poetry helps us appreciate what life is and how it can be lived. And it does all that by the use of words.

Sometimes, word choice can have a musical quality but not engage us. Compare the section of Coleridge's poem to this verse:

Roses are red and violets are blue.
Sugar is sweet and so are you.

Both lines rhyme. In the first line there is the alliteration of *roses* and *red* and the assonance of the *o* of *rose* and the *o* of *violet*. In the second line there is the alliteration of *sugar* and *sweet* and the assonance of the *a* of *and* with the *a* of *are*.

Yet in this verse, which seems to have been dashed off, there is no subtlety in the diction or in the meaning. There is neither depth of emotion nor depth of message. The singsong quality makes it shallow and somehow insincere. It sticks in our mind even though we don't want it to. In the Coleridge poem, the rhythms have an appealing flow. This becomes a mechanism by which we feel the poet's genuine sincerity, an intimate sharing in a precious moment between father and son, and we want to remember it.

Now we look at the first stanza of a famous eighteenth-century poem "Elegy Written in a Country Churchyard," by Thomas Gray. As we have seen, prose is about how words tell; poetry is about how words become euphony, music. The use of vowels is the main way that the pleasure of musical sound resonates in language. Notice how the poet so deftly achieves this:

> The Curfew tolls the knell of parting day,
> The lowing herd winds slowly o'er the lea,
> The plowman homeward plods his weary way,
> And leaves the world to darkness and to me.

The poet lines up all five vowel sounds with the *a*'s, *e*'s, *i*'s, *o*'s, and *u*'s, in both their long and short forms, subtly placed and certainly memorable. Vowel sounds are universally used to communicate to babies, to show excitement or awe, and to indicate sexual pleasure. They are the essential sounds of our most basic and uninhibited humanity.

Notice also how the poet immediately transports us into a reverie—as a lullaby does—by using so many *l*'s in the first stanza: *tolls, knell, lowing, slowly, lea, plowman, plods, leaves, world*. He adds to the pacific, whispering tone with *w* sounds: *lowing, wind, weary, way, world*.

The title uses two words to refer to the ending that is death: *Elegy* and *Churchyard*. An elegy is a poem that mourns a death or loss. A churchyard in that era was a burial ground. The very first line of the poem uses four of its six words to suggest endings: *curfew, tolls, knell, parting*. We also notice that the last line of the first stanza uses the words *leaves the world*. The words *slowly, plods,* and *weary* slow down the action and put us in a solemn mood, the very word used in the second stanza: "And all the air a *solemn* stillness holds."

The poet is doing what we can do with our own poems, finding consolation in a place of loss. He is holding us, as mothers do when they sing us a lullaby, so that we can ponder the mystery of endings. Good poetry offers just such disarming arms.

Gray's entire poem rhymes, and we notice that the rhyming is not forced or singsong, as in the verse about roses and violets, but natural. The poet has achieved a melodic mood that is pleasing as well as calming—in keeping with the elegiac nature of the poem. Ezra Pound wrote to poets, "Compose in the sequence of a musical phrase, not in the sequence of a metronome."

This poem was written in iambic pentameter, a fixed rhythmic pattern of syllables, and this adds to its musicality. An iamb is a two-syllable unit of rhythm in which the first syllable is unstressed and the second is stressed, as in the word *compare*. Pentameter means that there are five units of rhythm in a line, as in Shakespeare's "Shall I compare thee to a summer's day?" Iambic pentameter has a soothing quality, since this traditional meter also matches the natural breath breaks of English speakers. Japanese speech, by contrast, falls into breathing groups of seven and five, hence haiku poems use lines of five, seven, and five syllables. Meter is thus appealing as a body rhythm rather than an intellectual pleasure, which poems also offer. The rhythms of poetry are ultimately compelling because they remind us that we are composed of rhythms, and poems can mirror them back to us.

For many centuries, it seemed that writing was not poetry unless it was composed in iambic pentameter or in other formal examples of meter. Today poetry has freed itself from these binding obligations. We have learned to express rhythms without the need to adhere to an unswerving series of syllables and stresses. This is a major advance in the freedom of the poetic mind. Yet there will always be room for meter, since poetry is free to use anything in word, rhythm, rhyme, or mood to make its mark.

The poem by Gray lulls us by its theme, mood, and word choice. The following poem does the opposite. It is "The Battle Hymn of the Republic," composed by Julia Ward Howe to stir men to join the Union army during the Civil War. It was published in *The Atlantic Monthly* in 1862. Notice these two stanzas:

Mine eyes have seen the glory of the coming of the Lord;
He is trampling out the vintage where the grapes of wrath are
stored;
He hath loosed the fateful lightning of His terrible swift sword;
His truth is marching on.

He has sounded forth the trumpet that shall never call retreat;
He is sifting out the hearts of men before His judgment seat;
Oh, be swift, my soul, to answer Him! be jubilant, my feet; Our
God is marching on.

We see right away how the word choice in the two poems differs: Some words leave a trail behind them, making them pause rather than end. Such fading away fits the theme of Gray's "Elegy," so we have words that leave a wake of pleasing, quiet sound: *tolls, knell, day, slowly, lea, weary, way, leaves, darkness, me.*

In "The Battle Hymn," we have crisp, sharp-edged words that more easily make room for the word immediately following, with no pause in between. This is a word choice that matches the theme of moving, swordlike, without hesitation: *mine, seen, coming, Lord, trampling, vintage, grapes, wrath, stored, loosed, fateful, lightning, terrible, swift, sword, truth.*

"The Battle Hymn of the Republic" is not generally considered a great poem, but it cannot be matched for its skill in instilling a sense of propulsion. It has get-up-and-go in every line, impelling the listener to take action. Indeed, it did just that as it inspired men of the time to enlist in the Union army. Notice the number of motion words: *coming, trampling, loosed, fateful lightning, swift sword, marching on, never call retreat, sifting, be swift, be jubilant my feet, marching on.*

The hymn is also unparalleled in how it uses words and images with a startling power to arouse and encourage. The poet wrote it spontaneously, from sheer inspiration, all in one sitting. How fitting a comment on the American dream that Martin Luther King, Jr., would quote those same two stanzas, one hundred years later, in his own stirring speeches but applying them to nonviolence instead of war. This is the power of poetry, to cross the Mason-Dixon Line of the human heart.

Messages in Poetry

Some poems present a poet's real experience with no attempt to import a message. Others present a message unabashedly. As an example of the difference, we can compare the work of two poets.

The first poem is by Emily Dickinson, one of her best:

I heard a Fly buzz—when I died—
The Stillness in the Room
Was like the Stillness in the Air—
Between the Heaves of Storm—

The Eyes around—had wrung them dry—
And Breaths were gathering firm
For that last Onset—when the King
Be witnessed—in the Room—
I willed my Keepsakes—Signed away
What portion of me be
Assignable—and then it was
There interposed a Fly—

With Blue—uncertain stumbling Buzz—
Between the light—and me—
And then the Windows failed—and then
I could not see to see—

Here is a poem by Anne Bradstreet, entitled "In Memory of My Dear Grandchild Anne Bradstreet, Who Deceased June 20, 1699, Being Three Years and Seven Months Old":

With troubled heart and trembling hand I write.
The heavens have changed to sorrow my delight.
How oft with disappointment have I met

When I on fading things my hopes have set.
Experience might 'fore this have made me wise
To value things according to their price.
Was ever stable joy yet found below?
Or perfect bliss without mixture of woe?
I knew she was but as a withering flower,
That's here today, perhaps gone in an hour;
Like as a bubble, or the brittle glass,
Or like a shadow turning, as it was.
More fool, then, I to look on that was lent
As if mine own, when thus impermanent.
Farewell, dear child; thou ne'er shalt come to me,
But yet a while and I shall go to thee.
Meantime my throbbing heart's cheered up with this—
Thou with thy Savior art in endless bliss.

The poem by Emily Dickinson employs wry irony to show how our human solemnities are at the mercy of mundane realities, "a fly in the ointment" as it were. It seems that Emily Dickinson did not believe in the afterlife as it was conventionally understood. Hence we find her almost humorous parody of the serious leave-taking in which her friends are waiting for God (or Death), "the King," to enter the room and carry her soul to heaven. Instead, the ordinary housefly interrupts and can't be shooed away, royalty or no. The great occasion has become his moment, to be sure. The other-worldly light faded once attention was arched toward his fumbling buzz. The entrance of the fly represents the real arrival of death, as opposed to the version held by the onlookers, who see death as the majestic King.

The poet adds the extra "To see" in the last line to prevent us from thinking she now *sees* in some new, astral way. I think Emily Dickinson wants us to know of the finality of the death experience, the blind alley she is confronting. She is bravely searching the extremities just as they appear in her experience. A poet who was satisfied only with a silver lining of religious promise in human events might have ended the poem this way:

I could not see with mortal eyes—
But glimpsed divine surprise.
A fly is not too small to be
An angel in disguise!

However, it is the power of great poetry that a larger truth may still emerge in spite of the poet's belief system. An affirmation of a reality that transcends the poet's limited view might slip through to us. We see such transcendence happening in the poem. It contains, subtly, the following three chords of spiritual or transpersonal consciousness:

First, we notice a *combination of opposites* in *the King* and *a fly,* in the *stillness* and the *buzz,* in the held *breaths* of those gathered around the bed and the *uncertain stumbling buzz* of the intruder. The mourners are certain; the fly is uncertain—like faith and doubt. The combination of so many opposites is a sign that the transpersonal realm has entered the poem, just as it has entered the room.

Second, the dying woman wills her keepsakes and every portion of herself that can be given away. This is a letting go, so characteristic of threshold etiquette on the journey to wholeness. It reminds us of Meister Eckhart's words: "Everything is meant to be lost that the soul may stand in unhampered nothingness." Letting go is not ending but preparing.

Thirdly, the poem escorts us into the liminal world, the realm of the in-between: "There *interposed* a fly . . . *Between* the light and me." That certainly can symbolize the bridging of our mortal reality and a transpersonal world impervious to time's decay—but the poet is too professional in her craft to state that to us directly.

The Bradstreet poem, on the other hand, is straightforward in presenting a belief in the afterlife. The poet feels her faith as a consolation prize for the untimely death of her granddaughter. The poem has an agenda, as a sermon does. She tries, kindly, to help us believe as she herself does. Nonetheless, Anne Bradstreet does not *show* us the experience that led her to the last line of her poem. Her hope seems to be based on an a priori belief that she has applied to this recent experience.

Alternatively, Emily Dickinson states her experience by her bald description of the fly and her reaction to it, with no added recourse to a preexisting creed. The first poem tells us what the poet sees. The second poem tells us what the poet believes.

The Emily Dickinson poem is philosophical, confronting an existential issue and offering no clear solution. The Bradstreet poem is theological, also confronting an existential issue but with a tidy answer. It records an event that actually happened and finds comfort in faith for the future. The Emily Dickinson poem presents a future event as a metaphor. Her purpose is to open a subject and leave it open. She is letting us join her in being uncomfortable. Emily Dickinson is signaling to us that death, and perhaps all the ultimates in life, may not turn out to be what we expect.

Anne Bradstreet is memorializing an event that she actually experienced, the untimely death of a close relative and her consequent grief. She is using her poem to bring to us the comfort she herself found. Emily Dickinson is offering possibilities of how we might see our own death. Anne Bradstreet seems to be limiting the meaning of an experience to one reliable outcome, based on her firm religious perspective.

The quality of the poems is not the issue here, nor is the belief system of the poets. Both are legitimate. The Bradstreet poem seeks to soften the impact of death. The Dickinson poem lets us feel its thud. The comparison is between a bold description of experience with no a priori or comforting assumptions and a faith-based purpose in writing. Her poem simply declares; the other seeks to persuade and console too.

Some readers want to be persuaded. Yet, if Emily Dickinson believed in the afterlife, she probably would not have tried to convince us of her faith in any case. Some people want to be left to their own beliefs. If Anne Bradstreet had not believed, she might have tried to show us the legitimacy of that. She cares that we find what she has found. We sense—and can appreciate—a missionary zeal. Emily Dickinson simply opens us to what she found. We are left hanging, a legitimate description of our existential condition and of the realm of the in-between.

By comparing the two poems, perhaps we can now better see how a poem makes something personal the truth in the moment. In the objective world, only what can be proven or confirmed by reason and investigation is real. In a poem, the poet's world is real no matter how fanciful it may be. We can see that poetry has pluck.

Poetry enshrines experience. Poems are unique comments on reality and grant the reader an opportunity then to shape it as he sees and feels it. Even though poetry works best when it does not attempt to convince, there remains a place for the alternative. This is why both Emily Dickinson and Anne Bradstreet will always be read and appreciated.

Helpful Suggestions for Reading Poetry

Here are some specific hints that may help us find pleasure and meaning in reading a poem:

- Always reread. We usually have to "double-click" a poem to open it. We may have to read a poem many times to appreciate its point. Each rereading leads to more clarity and thereby increases our confidence as readers. When we stay with a poem, it yields more and more, something like staying with our own feelings to reach their authentic origins, motivations, and implications.
- Mindfully notice the feelings a poem arouses in you. Then look at the theme and story in the lines, individual phrases, and images, and finally, in specific words. Return to the theme to see how all the words and lines express and illustrate it.
- Remember that the ultimate goal is not to find out what a poem means or what question it answers. The purpose is to *let something in the experience of reading the poem come into focus for you, not only mentally but in an embodied way.*
- It is important not to look for a lesson or to expect to be consoled by finding a silver lining, unless that is the poet's intention. More often, a poem simply tells it as it is. Its purpose is not to cheer us up but to tell the truth, and if that is cheerful, *mazel tov.* If it is not, *amen.*

- Don't stop at the beauty of the words in a poem. Look for the meat, subject, mood, meaning, personal connotations—or any one of those.
- When the syntax in a poem is skewed and the grammar is off, pressure is being deliberately placed on the words. This is meant to reflect and/or create an emotional intensity in the reader. The poetic diction increases the power of what a poem is trying to convey. The sentence structure is meant for artistic effect, not adherence to logic. Notice all this as a witness rather than as a critic.
- Come to a poem in order to appreciate rather than to define. Poems often suggest rather than state, so do not put too much of your emphasis on interpretation.
- When you find a poem difficult to understand, try writing it out in longhand or typing it. You may find that this process sheds light on what it is about. An alternative is to give up trying to understand and simply enjoy the images and rhythms, join into the mood, feel the feelings in the poem.
- A joy in poetry is suddenly noticing likenesses we might never have imagined possible—metaphors make them visible. We begin to see how all things can commingle or even become one. For instance, love and wind do not seem related. But a metaphor describing our uniquely shaky bond with someone shows the two words can indeed fit together: "Our love is a bargain with the wind." Look for metaphors and appreciate their power to help us understand interconnectedness.
- If you are especially drawn to a poem and find a lot in it, write your own poem in response to it or as an extension of it in accord with your own life experience.
- Try writing a poem that copies the style of a poet you especially like or admire. This exercise helps you understand a poet better. In addition, you learn to write in a way that pleases you and shows you the scope of your own skill. (For an illustration, go to the third poem in the appendix called "Shakespeare in Oz." In this poem, for fun, I attempted to use Shakespeare's style to write a speech for the scene from the movie *The Wiz-*

ard of Oz. My poem is written in what is called mock heroic style, lofty language that is meant to be humorous.)

- Finally, beware of what happened to Charles Darwin. Here is a disturbing passage from his journal: "I have said that formerly pictures and also music gave me great delight. But now, for many years, I cannot endure to react to a line of poetry. I have tried lately to read Shakespeare and found it so intolerably dull that it nauseated me. I have also lost my taste for pictures and music . . . . And if I had to live my life again, I would have made it a rule to read some poetry and listen to some music at least once a week, for perhaps the part of my brain now atrophied would have thus kept active through use."

Lectio Divina

Lectio Divina is Latin for "divine reading" and refers to a monastic practice of reading the Bible in a meditative or prayerful way. The goal was for the reader to become open to receiving God's revelation on a personal level. This practice was customary in Benedictine monasteries as a way of cultivating skill in deep listening, hearing "with the ear of our hearts," as Saint Benedict suggested.

Before beginning, the practitioner calms his mind by taking deep breaths, letting go of plans and thoughts, and using a short prayer or affirmation for guidance. Openness to the voice of Spirit over ego is crucial to set the tone of the *lectio*. This means listening rather than thinking.

The Bible passage is chosen ahead of time. The practice is done in one hour or in two half-hour periods, morning and evening. By practicing at the same time each day, the habit becomes more easily ingrained and rhythmic. The place of practice is also the same, so that there are less distractions, since the setting is so familiar.

This practice, of Christian origin, can be adapted to anyone's life. The God within can be the Buddha mind or the archetype of the spiritual Self, or a Higher Power, or simply the depths of our own being. Spirit can be any reality that transcends ego. The metaphor of speaking and listening can refer to active imagination, in which a similar dialogue occurs. We will see more examples of these options in the practice that follows.

Guigo, a twelfth-century Carthusian monk, described four stages of *lectio divina:* reading, pondering, praying, and contemplating:

1. Reading

Using a brief passage from scripture, the practitioner reads slowly and reflectively, continually rereading when distractions interfere with his or her focus. The idea is to attune to a back-and-forth rhythm in the message, very like what we do in reading a poem. Attuning to the rhythm means that spiritual reading as an "activity" becomes a "receptivity." (This will, in a later phase of the practice, lead back to "activity" in the daily world.)

"Listening" is used in the same sense as in the Hebrew Bible phrase "Hear, O Israel! The Lord our God is one." In this call to prayer, the listening is not simply to understand that God is one, but that all is one, and that our behavior has to become one with our profession of faith. The word *listen* has thus an expanded meaning.

2. Pondering

In the second stage, the practitioner meditates on the passage, phrase by phrase, until it speaks personally to him. This pondering has been compared to ruminating, chewing the cud of meaning in the words, with no attempt to come up with an interpretation. The purpose is rather to see how the meaning applies to one's own life. A linear meaning is no longer primary. This is how the words become a voice that personally guides and uniquely reveals.

3. Praying

Pondering leads to the third stage of prayerful response in which the reader speaks to God directly in his own words as if in a conversation. The practitioner presents his most confusing problems, his most painful experiences, his doubts and hopes to God, who is also a Listener, so that a healing may arise from a word or phrase in the passage he has been reading. This is allowing the soul to be moved and transformed by a revelation that speaks to its here-and-now condition.

4. Contemplating

In the final stage, the practitioner enters restful contemplation. This is a wordless openness to being held in God's loving embrace so that he knows now, experientially, that God is love. He also opens to what God wants to say or work within his heart. There is a letting go of concepts, ideas, and even of the words of the scripture he has been reading. In such contemplation the practitioner simply lets be. Then he may sense a divine presence that accompanies him in daily experience. *Lectio divina* has now led to *presentia divina,* or divine presence.

This resting in the Word of God is a way of listening at the deepest level of being to the Spirit, who listens to the human within and speaks within. Openness to that voice is meant to have a lasting effect on the way one lives. This change is the best indicator of the authenticity and effectiveness of the *lectio divina* style of prayer. From an archetypal point of view, Spirit refers to the wisdom archetype in the higher Self.

Listening means that we are highly alert and deeply attentive. We have an innate capacity for this kind of listening and contemplation. A silence happens as we let go of words and thoughts, both externally and internally. We join this silence to stillness, which is a letting go of movement. This listening in silence and stillness takes us to what has been hidden under our thoughts, patterns, addictions, and our cultural and personal attachments. That hidden realm is Buddha nature, Christ consciousness, God within, our authentic self. This is how contemplative listening helps us transcend our ego. All it takes on our part is consent. We undermine the ego's hegemony over our minds and lives, and what arises in its place is our inherent goodness, serenity, joy, and equanimity. These fruits of our contemplation are what we bring to the world around us.

What has happened within the soul now infuses external activity and decisions. This is the completion of "attuning to the rhythms" mentioned above: Activity leads to receptivity, which leads to a new style of activity, new behavior in daily life, that puts the theme of the reading experience into practice.

EXERCISE

A Spiritual Approach to Reading Poetry

Try applying the four-stage technique of *lectio divina*—reading, pondering, praying, and contemplating—to the reading of poems that have meaning for you. Be sure to add the "change in behavior" feature if you want your practice to become a commitment in the here-and-now world.

Once a week, choose a poem that lends itself to your practice of this technique. It does not have to be overtly spiritual, religious, or lofty. Choose whatever speaks to you at a more intense level than the one where you might ordinarily find yourself, that is, the transcendent. Substitute affirmations for prayer if that is more appealing to you. Substitute dialogue with your inner self in place of God if that fits for you.

Dharma is the Buddhist term that refers to the truth about the way things are and the teachings that help us work effectively with them. Poems are Dharma texts in which we can take refuge. If you have a Buddhist practice, design the *lectio* to fit that frame of reference. God in that context can be Buddha mind, which is somewhat like God since it transcends ego.

The Psalms or a passage from the Bible, Buddhist Sutras, *Bhagavad Gita,* or any poem that strikes you as meaningful can be useful in this practice, no matter what your spiritual framework.

Write about your experience later in a poem of your own. Use that poem for *lectio* some other time. Begin your experiment by using the poem by Saint John of the Cross on pages 123–125, or one of the following two poems.

Here are the first four stanzas of "In No Strange Land" by Francis Thompson:

> O world invisible, we view thee,
> O world intangible, we touch thee,
> O world unknowable, we know thee,
> Inapprehensible, we clutch thee!

Does the fish soar to find the ocean,
The eagle plunge to find the air—
That we ask of the stars in motion
If they have rumor of thee there?

Not where the wheeling systems darken,
And our benumbed conceiving soars!—
The drift of pinions, would we hearken,
Beats at our own clay-shuttered doors.

The angels keep their ancient places—
Turn but a stone and start a wing!
'Tis ye, 'tis your estrangèd faces,
That miss the many-splendored thing.

Or, try this profound poem by Li Po, an eighth-century Chinese
Buddhist poet:

Now the last bird has vanished into the sky,
And the final cloud dissolves away.
We sit together, the mountain and I,
Until only the mountain remains.

Epilogue
Our Evolutionary Calling to Poetry

The aim of the poet and of poetry is finally to be of service,
to ply the effort of individual work into the larger work of
the community as a whole.

—SEAMUS HEANEY

Psychological health reaches its zenith when it
includes a spiritual consciousness that takes note of the world's condition and wants to make a contribution to its healing. The calling
to pay attention to poets of our time and to write our own poetry is
not simply personal. It is also collective and evolutionary. Evolution
proceeds as we commit ourselves to ever more imaginative ways of
connecting to the world around us. Sometimes this is accomplished
simply by communicating our concerns. A poem with universal
voice is a coin, a means of exchange at the level of the greatest human value.

Some ideas are personal, for instance, installing a security system
in our home. Some ideas are collective, for instance, abandoning
war as the solution to political problems or finding a cure for an
epidemic. Our genetic code influences our choices in life and can
become fuel for our poems. A collective code determines the for-
mation of our culture, energy that can arise in us for the writing of
poems that reach out to heal the world's suffering.

The calling to be a poet today is to find a code that turns us toward life so we can undo the death-dealing policies and choices that
make the world so dangerous and put it so at risk ecologically. This
is being true to life. The move toward life and higher consciousness is ever arising in our commitment to cocreate, to join with the

creative forces of evolution. Poetry is one form such passion can take. Every poem is a political and spiritual act. It becomes so by the uniqueness of the voice of the poet and his or her commitment to a better world. This is what André Malraux may have meant when he wrote, "Artists do not emerge from a formless world but from their struggles against the forms imposed by others."

Through poetry, our own and that of others, we discover the subtext of life as an *unus mundus,* to use the medieval phrase meaning "one world." This refers to the spiritually charged realization that there is no sharp division between mind and body, masculine and feminine, form and freedom, above and below, inner and outer, within and without, human and natural, sacred and profane. All is one just as poetry is one art though with manifold subjects. This mystery of "only-ness" may lie beyond the comprehension of linear reasoning. But it is ever energetically opening to poetic sensibilities. Poets, with their universal themes, help decipher the code of oneness so that the world's fulfillment can happen.

Our bodies are geared to knowing what to do when we are being born, getting sick, or dying. There is also an innate knowing in nature: heralding seasons, churning up earthquakes, displaying rainbows. We contain that same innate intelligence in our poetic imagination. A poet can pay attention to personal events in her own story or in that of nature, the news, or history. In each of these, life finds new forms, as do the poems that catch on fire because of them.

Our ordinary consciousness can write a poem that is personal, an insightful accomplishment. A higher consciousness in us can see that poem, and every poem, as an instance of enlightenment. In such a moment we realize our unique role in the story of the universe. Then we see that our soul's rhythms were always the same as those of the planets, the waves, and poetry.

Today's poet with social consciousness is still part of an ancient order of priests. In the past he made a pact with the darkness; now his task is to interpret the light.

—PABLO NERUDA, *Memoirs*

Appendix
Sample Poems

I.

Listening to Mothers
"I asked your Grandma once
I said Ma I still wonder
How you survived how you lived your days
All these years
After losing not one but two sons?"

"Louise, I think it was the *Pietà*
Where the Madonna, she shows
All us mothers who lost sons
How to go on living dying
You just keep holding them in your lap
All your life
You never bundle them away
And then somehow, after a long time,
Your heart stops breaking."

"David, wasn't that
An elegant answer?"

2.

Litany

Bursting Virgin, expect me
Mother most brooding, hatch me in time
Nurse of the pearl whey, press me to your breasts
Madonna of evening tenderness, hold me with both hands
Mistress of hearths, my shelter be
Escort of journeys, accompany me
Woman of mystery, make sense of me
Lady of light, see through me, see me through
Dame of the dark, clutch me in my abyss
Grandmother of sorrows, grieve with me
Queen of swords, slash me, scatter me
Rose of thorns, bud me bloom and blow
Maiden of meaning, deeply involve me
Bride of Shiva, wholly dissolve me
Goddess of sun and snow, chant in me your seasons:
Full of grace you and I
Now and at the hour.

3.

Shakespeare in Oz
[Glinda's final speech to Dorothy about returning home from Oz
imitating the style of Shakespeare]

Be not afear'd, thou art not stranded here,
Thou joy of Kansas, gift of Jove to us,
Whom timely cyclone pitched to our domain,
By choice or chance, to win us all from woe.
Thou art the sweet reluctant nemesis
My ill-starred sister faced in fiendish wrath
When, visage green with envious spite, she groaned
To see her slippers fit so firm on thee.
Hail, valiant pilgrim, rubied in thy worth,
Who with the shield Athena Perseus gave
Didst slay Medusa but wast not slain too.
Hail, grounding force of sky-borne monkeys who
Were once so cruel, now happy to be kind.
Thou didst recall the troops, not muster them
As tim'rous king, of crown unsure, will send
To far-off lands our bravest corps, his throne
To verify.   Beholden denizens
Of newly ransomed Oz give tender thanks
To thee and to thy scarred but rugged friends:
A scarecrow stuffed secure with caring wit,
A tin man blessed with heart and tears alike,
A lion bold to growl and stand up tall,
And most of all, thy winsome daring dog,
The little pilot of this whole crusade,
The selfless, loving, loyal boast and best,
Who drew the drape that hid the wizard's feint.
O'er all of you we pass our wand with grace,
And, as thou exit from this globe, we grieve
Like lonesome cygnets, who, with fretful sighs,
Will hark the dirge their mother croons at last

And nestle, rueful, nigh her downy breast,
Perchance her brooding feathers one more time
Might lull them as in bygone warm white days.
So cling we to our moment final here
With thee, and yet we have to let thee go
That thou mightst haste thy way to sepia lands
And sing again thy rainbow bluebird song,
The Orphic hymn that wakes dun Hades' drowse
And ushers souls to glimpse the prairie's glow.
No need for zeppelin hurled by fickle wind,
No need for bungling wizardry at helm,
No need for sulfur, magic, or for gong,
Great heart, you've had the power all along!

About the Author

DAVID RICHO, PhD, MFT, is a teacher, workshop leader, and psychotherapist in Santa Barbara and San Francisco, California. He combines Jungian, transpersonal, and mythic perspectives in his work. For more information, including events and audio programs, visit www.davericho.com.

Books and Audio by David Richo

Being True to Life: Poetic Paths to Personal Growth (2009). Becoming healthy, both psychologically and spiritually, includes releasing the full range of our imagination about who we are and can be. Writing poetry can be a surprising tool in that exciting venture. Using Buddhist and Jungian perspectives, this book offers a fresh and inspiring approach to personal growth, one that taps into our inherent creativity and the versatility of poetry. We who have never considered ourselves to be poets will feel empowered to give it a try and see what we can discover about ourselves and our world.

Making Love Last: How to Sustain Intimacy and Nurture Genuine Connection (2008). Intimacy is one of the great powers and joys of life, yet all too often it gets clouded by miscommunication, a loss of affection, and a lack of mutual support. In this audio program, David Richo shows us how to use mindfulness to increase our capacity to give and receive love, improve physical and emotional intimacy, resolve conflicts constructively, move from needy, ego-centered love to unconditional love, and discover how relationships can be a path to spiritual awakening.

Wisdom's Way: Quotations for Meditation (2008). This is a book of quotations gathered from a variety of sources in psychology and spirituality, especially Buddhist, Christian, Jungian, and transpersonal. The quotations are brief and can be used as springboards for meditation. They are divided into three sections: psychological insight, spiritual awareness, and mystical realization. And what's most notable is that the knowledge in this book is not foreign or even new. The wisdom of the ages is universal, immemorially enshrined in the depths of every human psyche.

When the Past Is Present: Healing the Emotional Wounds That Sabotage Our Relationships (2008). In this book, psychotherapist David Richo explores our tendency to transfer potent feelings about people from the past onto the people in our current relationships, whether they are our intimate partners, coworkers, or friends. This can become a major stumbling block in relationships, preventing us from seeing others as they really are. Richo offers valuable insights and practical guidance on how to recognize and free ourselves from this destructive pattern.

Everyday Commitments: Choosing a Life of Love, Realism, and Acceptance (2007). In this unique book, David Richo offers fifty-two promises we can make to ourselves to help us navigate the ups and downs of daily living in a wise, compassionate, and psychologically healthy way. Each commitment is followed by short, engaging commentary by the author. The book also includes practical exercises—including journaling, contemplation, and guided meditations—to foster inward growth and lasting positive change.

The Power of Coincidence: How Life Shows Us What We Need to Know (2007). Meaningful coincidences and surprising connections occur all the time in our daily lives, yet we often fail to appreciate how they can guide us, warn us, and confirm us on our life's path. This book explores how meaningful coincidence operates in our daily lives, in our intimate relationships, and in our creative endeavors. Originally published under the title *Unexpected Miracles,* the author has fully revised and updated the book for this edition.

The Sacred Heart of the World: Restoring Mystical Devotion to Our Spiritual Life (2007). This book presents a spirituality of heart based on the metaphor of the Sacred Heart of Jesus. David Richo explores the symbolism of the heart in world religious traditions. He then traces the historical thread of Christian devotion into modern times with a focus on the theology of Teilhard de Chardin and Karl Rahner to design a devotion that respects the new cosmology. This book may appeal both to Catholics as well as to people from other religious traditions.

Mary Within Us: A Jungian Contemplation of Her Titles and Powers (2007). In *Mary Within Us*, the Jungian archetype of the feminine aspect of God as personified by Mary is shown to be built into the design of every human psyche. This book is about the archetypal and mystical meanings in the titles of Mary in the universal Church since medieval times. *Mary Within Us* shows how we have always venerated not the literal Mary but the feminine dimension of the divine that she represents and enriches.

The Five Things We Cannot Change: And the Happiness We Find by Embracing Them (2005). There are certain facts of life that we cannot change—the unavoidable "givens" of human existence: (1) everything changes and ends, (2) things do not always go according to plan, (3) life is not always fair, (4) pain is a part of life, and (5) people are not loving and loyal all the time. Richo shows us that by dropping our deep-seated resistance to these givens, we can find liberation and discover the true richness that life has to offer. Blending Western psychology and Eastern spirituality, including practical exercises, Richo shows us how to open up to our lives—including to what is frightening, painful, or disappointing—and discover our greatest gifts.

How to Be an Adult in Relationships: The Five Keys to Mindful Loving (2002). "Most people think of love as a feeling," says David Richo, "but love is not so much a feeling as a way of being present." In this

book, Richo offers a fresh perspective on love and relationships—
one that focuses not on finding an ideal mate, but on becoming a
more loving and realistic person. Drawing on the Buddhist concept of mindfulness, *How to Be an Adult in Relationships* explores five
hallmarks of mindful loving and how they play a key role in our
relationships throughout life.

Shadow Dance: Liberating the Power and Creativity of Your Dark Side
(1999). Our "shadow" is the collection of negative or undesirable
traits we keep hidden—the things we don't like about ourselves or
are afraid to admit, but it also includes our positive, untapped potential. David Richo looks for where the shadow manifests in personal life, family interaction, religion, relationships, and the world
around us. He shows how to use the gentle practice of mindfulness
to work with our shadow side, and he provides numerous exercises
for going deeper.

When Love Meets Fear: How to Become Defense-Less and Resource-Full
(1997). We all construct walls so that people will not get too close
or love us too much. In *When Love Meets Fear*, Richo shows that
we can learn ways to let love in and to approach someone who
fears our love. He offers techniques that can release the scared ego's
hold-outs and hide-outs. As we enter gently into the jungle of fear
about love, loss, aloneness, abandonment, and engulfment, we become heroically defenseless enough to find inner resources so fear
can no longer stop us.

*How to Be an Adult: A Handbook on Psychological and Spiritual Integra-
tion* (1991). This is a handbook on how to become an adult who is
able to maintain a strong adult ego and simultaneously go beyond
it to release the spiritual powers of the Self. It is the heroic journey
of exploring our personal issues and finding ways to deal with our
childhood wounds, our need to be more assertive, our fear, anger,

and guilt. The book then looks at common issues—such as how to work with fear of closeness, how to increase intimacy, and how to set boundaries—so that we can be happier in our relationships. Finally, Richo looks at spirituality, unconditional love, and affirmations of wholeness.